Th

Therapy

A Guide to My
Recovery From Psychosis

Steve Colori

About the Author

Steve Colori was born in 1986 and grew up in rural Massachusetts. At age 19 while attending the University of New Hampshire he began losing his mental health and was first diagnosed with schizophrenia at age 22. Two years later his second and last episode occurred at age 24 and this time he was diagnosed with schizoaffective disorder. During the next several years of his life Steve worked hard with multiple forms of therapy to overcome the disorder. One of the most important therapies he used was writing therapy. He wanted to become a writer and decided to write a memoir which was paramount in his recovery from schizoaffective disorder and his advance beyond it.

Steve has published 20 First Person Accounts with Schizophrenia Bulletin by Oxford Medical Journals, he publishes fiction about mental health and stigma, and his memoir Experiencing and Overcoming Schizoaffective Disorder is available on

Amazon and Barnes&Noble and with multiple book sellers. Steve writes a column with The Good Men's Project titled Steve Colori Talks Mental Health which has been running since 2017. He has been published with Literally Stories, Talk Soup, Edify Magazine, The Flash Fiction Press, Short Tale 100, The Scarlett Leaf Review, A Story in 100 Words, Star 82 Review, and Adelaide Magazine. He has been lecturing Harvard Medical School's Resident Doctors quarterly since 2012 and he currently works as a Peer Specialist at McLean Hospital. Working full-time throughout the Psychotic Disorders Division he provides in-services for several units, he has didactics with Harvard Medical School's resident doctors regularly, he provides group therapy and peer to peer support, and he gives insight into mental health experiences. He also lectures at Simmons Graduate School of Social Work. Steve has lectured for Harvard Medical School's Executive Education Program; he has also lectured at Massachusetts General Hospital's Schizophrenia Day, NAMI's

Greater Boston Community Advocacy Network, and for the NAMI Reads program of Cook County Illinois.

One of the most important quotes he ever heard was "To Improve is to Change; to be Perfect is to Change Often" (Winston Churchill) and he has come to live by those words.

For years he has had a desire to help others through his writing and he still works hard towards doing so to this day. To read more of his work and to buy his first book, please visit SteveColori.com.

Table of Contents

Social Dynamics

Symptoms and Solutions

Living with Mental Health Struggles

Note From the Author

This is a collection of essays that I've written over the past several years, many of which are published whereas there are others that are new material. The essays contain a variety of techniques, ideas, understandings, and wisdom that I've personally applied to improve my mental health. These are things that have worked for me, which doesn't necessarily mean they'll work for everyone. There are recurring themes, as is the case with recovery, but new information unfolds within each reading. Each essay was originally written to stand alone, therefore I kept that format throughout so as to not take away from the integrity of each individual piece.

I want to thank everyone within my support network for all of their incredible help. I'm very grateful for the quality of life that I have today. I hope you find this book helpful whether you are experiencing mental health struggles, you're within someone's support network, you're a medical provider, or if you're just curious to learn more.

Social Dynamics

Social Skills and Psychosis: A Spectrum
Good Men Project, July 2019

During my first episode I was an English major and I read twenty books per semester for two years while developing psychosis. This led to a lot of the experiential side of schizoaffective disorder being tied into reading and writing. Analyzing my experiences with reading and writing have helped me to make great progress in becoming mentally and emotionally healthier.

At age twenty-five, one year after my second episode I decided I wanted to start pursuing writing. I started reading as much as I possibly could every day when I was supposed to be looking for a job. I wrote my first book but during the process I realized something critical. Reading fictional works and watching movies was a trigger for psychosis for me. When I stopped reading and watching TV and movies my psychosis abated. For the year I had been reading in preparation to write and the six months I did the writing my mind was spinning. I immediately noticed an improvement in my conscious thought, having a much clearer mind and I was able to speak to people again. I had gone days without being able to say much to anyone because the psychosis triggered from reading, TV, and movies disabled my ability to speak. My anxiety was lessened and I was able to function at higher levels and my executive functioning immediately improved. My nausea and headaches went away which I previously was not aware were a part of psychosis. I was excited when I figured out a way to limit some of my psychosis and I felt like I finally had a fighting chance.

Originally I thought this was going to be a huge burden and completely take writing off the table. However, I realized I wasn't triggered reading my own writing so I was still able to write which was a relief because it was something I really wanted to do. I decided I still had to read so I started reading poetry as I could read one or two poems a day and still ingest and analyze good literature. One of the major difficulties however, was how to lead a social life while not being able to watch any television or movies. At first it was painful when friends would ask me to go to a movie and I had to tell them I just wasn't interested. In this situation I was lying so that I didn't have to divulge personal information however, I wasn't aware that not divulging this information sent a negative message. Most people really enjoy movies and growing up my friends and

10

I always watched movies together. Deciding not to go with them in their minds seemed like I intentionally just didn't want to hang out with them. Avoiding social situations because of symptoms and trying to hide the symptoms created social isolation. For the past ten years people would talk about movies they liked or wanted to see and I would remain quiet for the entirety of the conversation. I think it was perceived as judgmental that I didn't want to talk to them about movies. For a while a part of me did really dislike movies and television partially because I couldn't watch and I was jealous but more so because they caused me symptoms and it was a scary thing for me to even talk about. Thinking and talking about the movies caused me to think of the symptoms they caused.

One of the important things I realized though was that if television, movies, and reading caused me such a high volume of symptoms they were an important area to analyze and dissect to improve the experiential side of my mental and emotional health. I learned if I wanted to make progress in becoming healthier this was where progress could be made. I analyzed how my experiences during my first episode as an English major correlated to my mental and emotional health. For the past seven years I've been working on fixing this problem and I've become a lot healthier. At one point I felt I had it fixed. It felt miraculous sitting through an entire movie without symptoms. The movie ended and I thought I was all right until I went to work the next day. One of the difficulties of psychosis is realizing that you're not functioning as well as everyone else, you're aware of it and they're aware of it, but you can't do anything about it. A two hour movie caused me two days of embarrassing neurosis where I was incredibly socially awkward, had a ton of anxiety, I was nauseous, and I had ear splitting headaches at random spurts during the day. This meant I had to get back to the drawing board. It became distressing thinking that movies were getting in the way of me having a social life.

As I progressed, I decided I wanted to become more open about my mental health. I was out with some friends at an indoor golf place and I told them movies caused me to see and hear things, which they occasionally do. I figured these would be the easiest and quickest symptoms to explain. These were friends who already knew about my diagnosis and I made this comment within the context of the conversation. Some of my friends were understanding while one thought he was the local psychiatrist.

He said," I don't see why that should affect you. Is it the lights? Is it the content? I dunno about this."

In this moment I felt discredited and invalidated. It was a courageous moment for me to even divulge that movies caused me all these problems and the immediate response was kickback. The friend thought he knew the answer to a problem I had been working on fixing for the past seven years. One of the most frustrating things though was that I wasn't able to give him a direct answer as to why movies and television cause me psychosis. To this day I don't know the answer but I was too embarrassed in the moment to tell him that I don't know why. My thought is that it's probably a complex web of thoughts that are interconnected because I've made progress on it but the problem still remains. This is the most difficult part of psychosis. You're consciously aware of what affects you and how it affects you within social situations but you don't know why. People like to drop comments in conversation and give you advice on how to become more functional at random times but they don't realize the depth of the issues. It's incredibly distressing when people do this and sometimes just makes things worse. It's like throwing a bucket of water on top of an iceberg and expecting the whole iceberg to melt. They can only see the distress on the surface but don't realize how much more is below the surface.

The other part about social awkwardness and neurosis is that people don't realize it's from past traumas and fears that are still within the unconscious mind. I had social difficulty in middle school to the point of nearly committing suicide and also in college during my first episode of psychosis. The average person might feel fairly safe in a social setting but for years I felt it was a dangerous place so there's a disconnect here. As I started plucking fears and insecurities about socialization from my unconscious mind and making them into zeros I started becoming less socially awkward. One of the major stressors I had within conversations was a direct result of knowing my social awkwardness was from my mental illness but not wanting to tell anyone and also being afraid people knew about my mental illness because of my awkward behavior. As I neutralized increasingly more fears around socialization and learned the rules of socialization my symptoms of psychosis decreased and along with that my social skills improved. For me there's a direct correlation between the number of social anxieties and fears I had and later got rid of equating to the ability to effectively socialize and my level of health within a conversation. It's a spectrum. This resulted in my social life improving and my mental and emotional health improving along with it for an innumerable number of reasons.

As I became healthier, (but still wasn't able to watch movies), I realized the inability to watch movies was not the barrier to my social life. As my mental health improved increasingly more people wanted to hang out with me and I learned that most people don't care about whether I can or can't watch movies. We found other things to do together. I think for me when I was less healthy and experiencing a higher volume of psychosis I didn't see things as clearly. I blamed my inability to socialize on not being able to watch television and movies as opposed to realizing that people didn't care so much about not being able to do those things. I think part of it was painful to realize I just wasn't functioning as well as everyone else to be able to interact with them on the same level. Once my social skills improved, which I did a ton of work on, people hung out with me regardless of not being able to watch movies.

Linguistics in Psychosis

Good Men Project, April 2019

Using human experience language has been an essential part of getting healthier. It shapes the way I look at myself and the way I interact with others as a peer and in my life away from my mental health.

I originally began using diagnostic terms thinking it was easier to separate myself from schizoaffective disorder. At first this was really helpful and gave me some space and understanding that there was some biology behind what I was going through. However, as time progressed, I've moved further away from diagnostic labels. When I started as a peer specialist I introduced myself by divulging my diagnosis. I wanted to give people a sense of what I had been through and I thought disclosing the diagnosis would open up conversation. As opposed to being a conversation starter, it made me nervous to disclose the diagnosis and I have since moved away from doing so. A supervisor also mentioned that everyone may have similar symptoms however the reasons they manifest can be different for everyone because we all have different experiences leading into our mental health struggles so diagnostic terms may not be helpful to use. It also shut down some conversations, while other people were really fascinated and resonated with what I had said by mentioning they have the same diagnosis. I think in the context of a conversation it has been important to talk within diagnostic terms if that's what the person wants to do and to honor the language each person decides to use for their self. I found a lot of useful work I've done has been de-stigmatizing the labels of mental health diagnoses for myself and for others.

When I was first hospitalized I remember having a number of worries and concerns about how my life would turn out based upon the original label of schizophrenia which was later categorized as schizoaffective disorder. There was so much popular culture stigma around schizophrenia when I was diagnosed with it that I was terrified of just hearing the word and never wanted to use it. The stigma surrounding the diagnosis originally gave me unnecessary concerns and worries that I would wind up being like some of the people in movies or on the news who had been given the diagnosis. I eventually realized that the diagnosis is just a generalized label for some of the cognitive and emotional cause and effect issues I had been having from trauma I had been through. When I finally realized this, a great deal of worry dropped off the table thus improving my mental health. Now, I just tell people that I've had mental health struggles and I was hospitalized at the same hospital I work at eight years ago. It's been a lot easier on my mental health to avoid talking too intensely about my diagnosis and to use language that moves towards recovery. I like to inform others as well that they don't have to speak in diagnostic terms and they can humanize the experiences they've been through thus humanizing themselves. As a person, I am Steve and mental health stuff is just something I have to deal with. I don't define myself based upon my diagnosis and symptoms and it's been liberating when I take this angle. On the contrary when others try to categorize me within diagnostic labels it feels marginalizing and secluding for many reasons. When the label becomes the person, this is when I feel I'm being categorized such as someone saying he's a schizophrenic, as opposed to he's someone who has dealt with schizophrenia. The other facet of this is I only deal with symptoms periodically throughout the day so it's not constant and it's not accurate to label someone by their diagnosis.

Outside of work no one knows about my diagnoses however, the second I have mentioned the word schizophrenia to folks conversations can shut down. Away from work if I'm not working on my mental health I'm just living my life and not necessarily thinking about my symptoms or experiences so looking at someone through the lens of a diagnosis does not give an accurate picture of who they are. Not having an accurate picture of someone can frame the way we think about them in a frame they don't look at their self through and there can be a disconnect in therapeutic contexts. I think it's been helpful for my own recovery to look at myself through a non-mental health lens and it feels normalizing, as I've had so many experiences that made me feel marginalized. I had to do a lot of work on establishing equality for myself with others after years of having felt I was different or subservient which is not the case. Establishing equality came in the form of journaling and just making realizations surrounding my equality to everyone else who does not have mental illness.

There are certain phrases I hear that make me cringe such as mental illness and chronically ill. If no other words fit the sentence I myself may use the term mentally ill however chronically ill are words that need to be removed from your mental health vocabulary. I almost always like to use language such as mental health struggles, working towards getting healthier, going through a tough time. I've found when I'm using language that moves towards recovery it creates inclinations to do things to improve my mental health and also for others to do so too. Positive language around mental health helps remove the stigma that mental health struggles are forever because as I'm beginning to learn increasingly more they are not. I started out seeing and hearing things, having disorganized thinking, not being able to speak, and sleeping twelve hours per day and I now have a full life where I own a home and work full time. I think a big part of my recovery has been the belief that others have had in me, which I eventually adopted, that I can and will get healthier. Language plays a big role in this.

The other concern with language can be when people are overly conscientious and overly concerned for my well-being. I know they mean well but it feels marginalizing when someone is treating me as if I'm fragile when I know I'm just as durable as anyone around me. I'll be the first to say there can never be too much kindness in the world and if this is your general nature towards everyone this is great and will definitely work in a therapeutic setting. However, I suppose sometimes when people are being uncharacteristically kind to me when they don't demonstrate that same kindness to others feels stereotypical. I think an overlooked part of interacting with anyone who has had mental health struggles is realizing they are a person first. Person first care means that people are fully aware of what they have gone through and they know the gravity of the situation. I find the overly kind approach creates a power dynamic of the helper and helped when I know I'm fully capable of helping myself. I know I really appreciate going out with friends and having them treat me the same way they would treat everyone else and I feel the same way when I'm in a therapeutic setting. This includes if they're making fun of me and holding me accountable to the same standards, positive or negative, that they're holding everyone else to. When people seem overly concerned for my well-being it feels patronizing. I think the way to not be patronizing is to put yourself in the person with lived experiences shoes and to have mutuality with them. When people were originally overly kind to me I thought I should treat myself a similar way and sometimes we adapt the treatment others direct towards us on ourselves. I think being overly cared for made me overly sensitive in moments and I had to unlearn being so overly caring towards myself to think more clearly and to make better decisions.

Self-Discipline and Positive Self Talk

Good Men Project, September 2019

During middle school, I received a lot of emotional abuse which I also saw as a harsh means of discipline. Whenever I said anything wrong or did anything differently there were people there to make harsh comments. Part of their anger was habitual and part of it could have just been trying to fit in. If the lead bullies were saying these things it was better for everyone else to join them than to become a target. An alliance with the seemingly stronger party was a means of safety for my classmates. Unlearning some of this pseudo-discipline became helpful in later years to improve my mental health and to alleviate this burden.

I talk a lot about discipline because in years after my episodes I was fairly socially awkward and a lot of this came from having learned thought patterns of self-abuse from others as a means of self-discipline which I had to unlearn. I was looking for ways to change my behaviors so that I could be kinder and to socialize better with everyone and this abusive self-discipline always seemed to be an automatic response in this effort. One of the most important things I had to realize in later years was that discipline was not supposed to be punitive. After having spent years of getting harshly rebuked even after making the slightest of mistakes, I had a tendency to provide self-punishments in my own internal monologue in the form of insults and sharp comments towards myself. Some might refer to this as negative self-talk. I was incredibly hard on myself in situations where I didn't need to be and also projected this behavior onto others. I had the thought that in earlier years in order for me to be disciplined it required the sharp words of others to keep me in line. Also, in later years I was living in a bubble of fearing my emotions. Whenever I did or said anything wrong I had overly strong negative emotional reactions and it was incredibly painful to make mistakes.

Thinking more on discipline, I began drawing some parameters for my own well-being and realized the purpose of discipline is strictly educational. Some folks may believe that discipline needs to be painful in order to be effective but for myself I've found the best modifier of behavior has been education and kindness. I found that many times in malpractices within discipline there is an element of retribution involved. Retribution in discipline caused me a lot of problems and I came to realize that dis-

cipline is strictly supposed to help not harm, otherwise it's not discipline. This element of retribution
from the disciplinarian, that being myself at times
and also others, comes from feeling an emotional
deficit. There's a comparison that was made where
someone else did something wrong but still felt better emotionally than the person who had been
wronged therefore their emotions needed to be
knocked down to the level of the person who had
been done wrong. This type of abuse which gets
mistaken for discipline only causes for reciprocal
abuse and interpersonal problems.

I originally thought I had to cause myself
and others pain to get them to do the right things
but after years of compounding my issues I found I
needed a more humane and also more effective
way of changing behaviors. In times where I didn't
necessarily have my heart in the right place a part
of it was from having a self-disciplinary method
where I would say mean and painful things to myself after making mistakes. Doing this created a lot
of pressure to succeed at everything I was doing.
Having this pressure created stress and caused me
to make more mistakes and also amplified my
symptoms. This disciplinary method was also projected upon others when I thought they were out of

line which got me in trouble from time to time. I was struggling to do and say the right things because I was afraid of myself. I realized that living in fear of my own self-punishments was a type of prison that was restricting my actions. Fear is a great inhibitor and as long as I was doing things out of fear instead of love my life would not be lived as freely as it could be. When I switched my disciplinary methods to be educational as opposed to abusive and painful it helped improve my mental and emotional health. I had to unlearn all the harsh abuse I had received over the years from myself and others and make the realization that I didn't need to hurt or harm myself emotionally, mentally, or physically in order to do and say the right things. I also had to unlearn the cruelty that was labeled as discipline from times that came from pledging a fraternity. I had to draw a line between what is educational and what is cruelty, realizing that discipline is not a place for cruelty even though it is commonly found there. I learned the way others had been trying to discipline me through harm over the years by ways of emotional, physical, and verbal abuse was wrong and also was completely ineffective. When discipline was punitive and painful it caused more problems and compounded my issues as opposed to solving the original issue and making me a better person. When I started asking myself what do I need to say to myself to learn and to grow as a person, particularly in social situations, I found my emotional burden was lifted. When I treated myself with kindness and self-compassion I was able to solve interpersonal issues much more easily than otherwise. Without the burden of fearing punishment every time I spoke it became a lot easier to speak and I found it easier to say and do the right things socially. This decreased my social anxiety immensely. I still had awkward moments and a part of that was learning more about socialization but it became a lot easier to learn and to teach myself when I wasn't living in fear. Not living in fear gave me an allowance for mistakes and having this self-allowance for making mistakes loosened me up which helped give me space to think. Having this space to think improved my emotional well-being and my social interactions immensely.

Conversational Differences Between Therapy and Life

After having been in therapy for several years, I didn't realize that therapeutic conversations were different than all my other conversations and this was creating a number of issues for me that I wasn't aware of. In retrospect, having established the differences in these conversations would have helped my social life immensely. This problem initially manifested for me because for the first year or so after my second episode the only conversations I was having were therapeutic. Aside from meeting with my doctor once per week, I was talking with very few people in very short snippets.

In therapy, I was habituated to divulging anything and everything personal, and in my social life I didn't establish within my mind what I should and shouldn't talk about. There were many instances where I disclosed information about myself that was far too personal and made people feel uncomfortable. Along with making them feel uncomfortable I also felt uneasy and initially I didn't know why. I had a standard of wanting ubiquity in everything in my life but I had to realize this just wasn't the nature of life. I was used to the therapeutic establishment where anything and everything was okay to talk about whereas in life away from therapy this is not the case. There was a part of me that was trying to make everything in my life normal to talk about, but I had to realize that sometimes normalization is not good. Sometimes, certain subjects haven't been normalized for good reason within particular social contexts. Knowing time and place, or relativity, was an essential component to understanding which conversational topics were good to talk about for any given conversation. There were many times I introduced subjects to talk about, not realizing that I was making people feel incredibly uncomfortable. Some of the awkwardness came from people not wanting to talk about my personal life and cause me embarrassment when I thought the things I was sharing were normal. As normal as they might have been for everyone to encounter individually, talking about them in certain settings just wasn't appropriate. I didn't have the insight to discern what was a socially acceptable topic in public, with groups, or in private. I thought anything and everything was okay to talk about at any time. However, when I learned this, I realized the quality of my conversations began to improve.

A part of me over the years has always been very curious intellectually, so naturally I wanted to talk about things I could learn more about. However, I had to realize this isn't the case for everyone and I also had to understand that I don't need to be constantly growing and improving. Some social situations are strictly for fun and should be kept that way and when they're not it can be distressing to others who are just trying to relax and have a good time. Knowing the context of a social situation and the purpose of it as well meant knowing that people don't always want to talk about problems. Many times, people are out to socialize and relax to get away from problems. This was difficult for me to comprehend initially because I was constantly working on improving my mental health. A part of this came from the multitude of issues I had to work on and the fact that many of the issues were interpersonal and behavioral as well. So naturally, social situations had become learning opportunities for me, which in part was good but I had to know when to just internalize this as opposed to drawing people into my problems when they didn't need to be drawn in and they didn't want to be either. I had to learn that people don't always want to hear about my problems and it's not always appropriate to share them. Some of what makes a situation relaxing is that it can be problem-free, such as in Hygge. Keeping conversations and fun events problem-free was an important skill I learned to improve my social life.

Another issue I encountered was that I was also trying to solve everyone else's problems, which created some space between myself and my peers. I had to learn that I'm not a mental health professional outside of work and that people don't always want to talk about their issues with me. I also had to learn that it's not my duty or responsibility to draw out people's issues, especially in social contexts. As my perception improved and I was able to see more of what was happening within social situations I had to learn how to let things go and to not divulge everything I knew. I learned that life is not a competition to share everything you've figured out and to know things that others don't and be the one to share them with everyone. Being perceptive meant being responsible and not sharing what I was able to figure out. I had to learn the purpose of perceptiveness is helping others, and if sharing my perceptions wasn't helpful then I should just keep them as mental notes in my mind.

Utilizations of Therapy

During my recovery process from schizoaffective disorder, there have been a number of things I do in therapy and in journaling to help myself recover. My process began when I wrote my memoir and had a chronology of all the traumatic experiences I had ever been through. Writing the memoir was fun but it was also difficult delving into all those dark memories. It took several years of work to address my issues one by one.

When I'm deciding what to address and what to work on I usually have to go with the issue that is in the way. There have been times where I wanted to work on stuff from middle school and/or problems other than the ones I had before me but I had more pertinent life issues that had to be resolved first. Resolving the issue that has been in the way has taken me down paths and to truths I never expected to learn, but it's been the most effective way of dealing with my trauma. There were many times I uncovered truths and found problematic ways of thinking unintentionally, just by going in the direction that has the most emotional salience and not always working on the things I specifically wanted to at times.

Many times, I have felt overwhelmed so when this occurs I just choose any issue I can really find a resolution for and resolve it. From there I tend to take a path to eventually get to the heart of the main issues I've been experiencing and find a way to alleviate their burden. Issue resolution and the most salient traumas I have in my mind have tended to dictate what I'll write about at times and also what I'll journal about. As a writer there has been a ton of growth as a person and the two have gone hand-in-hand. Writing has helped improved my mental health while improving my mental health has helped me to write more effectively.

While working on improving my mental health the first thing I'll work towards is feeling deserving of good mental health. To do this I inform myself that I would want everyone else including myself to be healthy and recover from the things I'm suffering from and that we're all working together. Sometimes this can be difficult and I've noticed when I'm really struggling with an issue I can think in circles. For me this is a good indication I'm up against something that is pretty scary for me to face and might be good to approach slowly or to go to my doctor for help or go to a friend or family member.

During journaling one of my main focuses is to increase my knowledge base about life and to gain wisdom. Doing so has given me insight into my own life and has helped alleviate many burdens. A part of my therapy has been developing my thoughts on issues like forgiveness, love, friendship, justice, and themes that have been prevalent in my recovery. For example, developing my knowledge base on issues such as justice has helped me to dispel notions of retribution and vengeance and this helped me to better understand the people who had done me wrong during my episodes. Getting rid of retribution and vengeance opened the gates to forgiveness. For years, before learning to forgive everyone for their wrongs I had a lot of anger and hatred and it was emotionally painful. Allowing myself to let go of what others had done to me allowed me to move on and also to reconnect with some people from my past I originally didn't want anything to do with. I think forgiveness is important for both others and ourselves. I don't think I ever would have arrived at this point had I never worked towards developing my thoughts on abstract subjects which eventually had practical uses in my recovery.

Another thing I do in therapy is setting directions for myself on how I want to be in social situations and how I want to treat others. During this process it hasn't been as simple as just telling myself that I want to treat others well when they make mistakes or have been mean to me, although this is the type of thing I write in my journals. It also has entailed unlearning bad behaviors and ways of treating others. This unlearning has been a process of delving back into the times where others had treated me poorly and evaluating whether that was a good way for those people to treat me, regardless of whether I was right or wrong. When making these evaluations I have come to realize that although I was wrong at times, I did not deserve to be treated so poorly by others. Unlearning bad behaviors has improved my overall mental and emotional health and has helped me to be more socially adept and functional within conversations of all types. I also had to unlearn behaviors from middle school trauma and other traumatic times. There were times in middle school where I would say the wrong thing and people would tell me I should kill myself. Looking at this from a logical standpoint, I would say that the reaction was not equal and opposite to me having said the wrong thing therefore I did not deserve to be told to kill myself and that I don't want to treat anyone this particular way. Establishing these axioms has dispelled the fears I had from these experiences and also has helped me to not repeat the same behaviors towards others.

One of the final things I do in journaling is to logically evaluate situations happening in my life and find solutions that will improve my overall well-being. This type of therapy has been less psychoanalytical and more so just practical, logical thinking about my life. A good portion of this can entail problems that are not psychological such as how to manage my money. However, I've realized that having real life issues on top of having schizoaffective disorder can tend to amplify those life issues while simultaneously amplifying some of the symptoms. Therefore when I have been able to find logical solutions to my life problems and situations it has also helped tremendously with my mental health.

Morality with Schizoaffective Disorder; A Cause and
Effect System
Good Men Project, April 2019

After two episodes of schizoaffective disorder and six years of living with the disorder I was
deeply concerned with morality and its connection
to my experiences. I knew I was a good person
who had just experienced The Book of Jobe, however, I still had feelings that the illness was my fault.

This was a tremendous burden to bare because it meant I had to have done something incredibly wrong to cause all the adversity I had
faced. I thought if "everything happened for a reason and I just went through two episodes of
schizoaffective disorder, I must be a terrible
person". I thought I must have done something to
deserve this.

During my episodes I tried as much as I
possibly could to keep to a strict moral code thinking it would help me to overcome schizoaffective
disorder. Having a good work ethic and good
morals helped but I was mentally rigid in the fact
that I wouldn't deviate or bend the slightest bit from
my notion of morality. This mental rigidity carried on
into the years after my episodes and I perceived

the world strictly from a moral standpoint. It was a sickness to be mentally rigid and was detrimental in my recovery.

Only in recent years have I come to realize that morality is not some omniscient magical force, that morals are rules decided on by human beings. Their purpose is to create positive results in one's own life and in the lives of others. This new understanding of morality helped me to decide when it was okay to bend or even break a rule, and when it was important to adhere to the rules. Of course that did not allow me to justify means that were immoral.

However, knowing I could deviate from my morals if there was no harm caused in doing so helped me to realize that I had flexibility within morality and it lessened my mental rigidity sur-rounding morality. While I still always weigh the consequences of each action before acting, that is different than just strictly adhering to what I've been told. This helped me to cater actions to situations instead of applying a one-size-fits-all morality.

Moreover, I now understood why bad things can happen to good people. I used to have the be-lief that if I did everything correctly from a moral standpoint that good things would always happen to me. I think this vantage point was instilled in me from years of watching TV and movies where good things always happen to good people and bad things to bad people. The thing I realized was that having schizoaffective disorder was largely biological which wasn't my fault. The illness was not caused by a moral failure on my part. Likewise, joining a fraternity may not have been helpful, but that poor decision was not an immoral act. I used to search my conscience for things I did wrong. I used to pray for forgiveness hoping that would get rid of the illness. The thing I came to realize was that I just wasn't strong enough to overcome the adversity of schizoaffective disorder in its initial onset. I was a good person but the cause of schizoaffective disorder happening went beyond morality. It was something morality couldn't predict or prevent and it was something where my biology and circumstances were two scientific causes that came together to make a terrible thing happen to a good person. There was no omniscient retribution system that was paying me back for something I'd done wrong as a kid. I was not to blame for my condition.

Moving forward the thing I realize that morals did play an important part in my recovery. Experiencing two episodes of schizoaffective disorder and recovering from them was constant adversity and I constantly looked to my moral compass to search for ways out of storms I wasn't certain how to navigate. The disorder was very disorienting mentally; therefore I had to rely on character to get me through the toughest times. Having good character with a good moral compass helped me to make decisions that created positive effects which helped me to recover from the disorder. Realizing that morality is a cause-and-effect system which serves people to create the greatest good for themselves and for others helped me to put my morals to better use. When I finally had an understanding of why morality is so important and why it works this helped me to better execute my morals. Growing up I was told to do the right thing but I was never told why. Knowing that there are reasons why we need to do what is right helped me to understand how to do it better and it also helped me to decide upon what is or isn't morally right or wrong. There are instances where there can be two correct decisions, however, when I knew the purpose for which I was making the decision (the desired effect), it helped me make a better decision as to which action would better create the desired effect. Finding a true north for my moral compass helped me to guide my actions with a purpose instead of blindly just doing what I thought was the right thing and hoping for a good outcome.

I also realized that morality works because it is a cause and effect system however, there are also times when things don't work out. Sometimes when things don't work out this is independent of morals. I learned that sometimes when bad things happen to me it might not be a question of morality at all or of how good a person I am or am not. I don't feel guilty anymore when bad things happen to me when I did nothing to cause them when in the past I used to feel some form of guilt if something bad happened to me regardless of the cause. For example I can see now if someone rear-ended me in a car accident it had nothing to do with how good or bad a person I was that day. It has everything to do with the fact that that person might have just been distracted and wasn't able to stop in time. The fact that they hit me might not be a question of morality at all. Maybe someone forced them into my lane at the last second or they skidded on a patch of ice. The point for me was that some things happen because of cause and effect and have nothing to do with how good a person I am or am not, such as having schizoaffective disorder.

Minimizing the Effects of Social Traumas

Good Men Project, April 2019

In recent years there have been some social traumas I've been working through from years
of being bullied. I have several groups of friends I
hang out with but I've realized I struggle to connect
with them and to hang out with them regularly at
times. There are some practices I adopted to pro-
tect myself from past social traumas which have
been causing me to isolate myself from others. During middle school and during my first episode of
schizoaffective disorder, I lost all my friends and I
realized I have been doing things to keep people
distanced from me to prevent this from happening
again along with the pain from these experiences to
recur.

The belief that I would lose all my friends
again was backed by strong and dark emotions
from having experienced this unfortunate occur-
rence twice in my life. It was really painful in middle
school and I nearly committed suicide and it was
really painful in college and it contributed to my first
episode. I learned that I made a lot of assumptions
that people automatically wouldn't like me or that I
would lose friends again or that my current friends

were not great friends. I many times talked myself out of making an effort to connect with people in order to keep them at distances from me. I was constantly worried about making friends that I would lose, so when new people I had met would invite me to do new things I usually declined. I didn't want to make friends with people whom I was afraid would abandon me.

I eventually realized that if I didn't at least make an effort to make friends and be susceptible to losing friends again that I would just be alone which was not what I wanted. I learned that if I didn't allow myself to be vulnerable in social situations there would not be room for any relationships to be fostered. There also wouldn't be room for me to grow as a person because without risk growth does not happen. I learned I had to take the risk of making new friends and allowing people to be close to me again. Letting people close to me has probably been one of the most difficult things about having gone through social traumas and schizoaffective disorder. Deep down I really want to have some close friendships and relationships but there are fears in the way which have caused me to keep people at distances and to not fully connect with others. A number of these fears are directly related to social traumas I experienced in middle school and during my episodes of schizoaffective disorder and I've been working to get rid of those chains so that I could be free to make friends again and allow people into my life.

I recently was hanging out with some friends and they were talking about their plans for the next day while I was there. I was too afraid to ask why they weren't inviting me and I got angry. They were going hiking and I wanted to go too or at least be invited along. I assumed they just didn't like me and they were being rude right in front of me. We had been watching sports games at my house when they didn't have cable so I also assumed they had just been using me so they could see the games. I sent a text the next morning out of anger and I got a response I didn't expect.

My friend informed me that she was searching for a condo two hours away and afterwards her and her boyfriend were going hiking. She told me she just didn't ask me because she assumed I didn't want to wake up early and wait for them to condo shop for two hours and then go hiking. My fear of people using me had been so salient from past years that it had caused me to assume the wrong thing about my friends. They wound up inviting me out the next day with another group of friends of theirs and forgave me for making a wrongful assumption. The thing I learned was to ask questions before I made poor assumptions and got mad at people. Doing so has kept me out of some trouble recently. I learned it's okay to ask questions and people respond well to questions but when I made bad assumptions about them and accused them of using me I of course was not creating good friendships. I learned people are open to questions in these types of situations if they're worded right but accusations tend to cause arguments and distance between people which was not what I wanted.

Mutuality; Making a Bully a Friend

Dealing with bullying has been an ongoing battle in my life that I feel I've finally gained some ground on. During middle school I was picked on to the point of nearly committing suicide, which eventually lead to mental rigidity thus causing schizoaffective disorder. Being bullied was a central theme in my recovery from schizoaffective disorder and was very painful to dismantle.

When I first started broaching the subject of my middle school years it was far too intense and painful of a complex to face head on. I could feel the emotional salience in my heart as it pained me even to think the smallest of thoughts about middle school. There were central issues and central bullies I wanted to address to find alleviation from all the pain I still felt at age 32 from my middle school experience. However, when I tried to resolve the bigger problems first, it was overwhelming and I wasn't able to do it. It caused immense emotional pain and was a real battle. Although I wanted to address the main issues I figured out I had to solve the problem in the way. Facing my most immediate problems regarding bullying eventually allowed me to access the bigger problems. Picking at the little problems and knocking them down is like running far distances. If you try to run nine miles your first time out it's overwhelming and you fall flat. If you build up to it and run one step at a time, focusing your energy on taking the best stride you can with each stride, you become better at running, and eventually you can run longer distances in shorter times. This is the same way working with mental health complexes works. The better I became at taking the smaller steps the easier it made it for me to go further distances into my psyche to get to the bigger issues. I originally utilized these skills in the beginning of my recovery when facing issues of schizoaffective disorder. As I grew older I worked my way backwards to middle school trauma but that same set of skills is transferrable.

One of the key components in the way for me to overcome my mental and emotional struggles from middle school was forgiveness. I had to remember all the instances where people had treated me poorly and figure out the social construct. I originally started journaling "I forgive BULLY X for telling me to kill myself and I still want to treat them well. Be Nice about this". Forgiveness has been the greatest medicine in my mental health recovery. I've had the same medication for eight years but some of the most drastic changes in my mental health have been a result of journaling about forgiving others in a heavy volume. I originally went through a list of the easiest things to remember about having been bullied, like being told to kill myself by everyone, and I forgave everyone for it. Forgiveness to me means hoping that someone has a good life despite what they did to me and they don't feel an emotional burden from it. It seems ironic that I wanted this for people but I realized after my mind became clearer that we were all bullying each other and we were all equally afraid growing up. I learned that behaviors I thought were joking towards others might have been damaging and the same behaviors were reciprocated towards me. After I began forgiving people this lightened my emotional baggage. With less emotional baggage I was able to see more clearly and travel further distances in dissecting my middle school experience. The next step was to get into social constructs and figure out what were the social constructs I had learned, which were maladaptive, that I needed to unlearn. This revolved around not blaming myself for other people's aggression, forgiving people for yelling at me and blaming me for their mistakes, forgiving people for treating me poorly, and there was also a lot of self-forgiveness involved.

Another important construct was that hurting and killing other people was not going to alleviate my mental and emotional burden. I mention killing because when I got home from school I would play first person shooter games on the worst days and take out my aggression within the video game. However this process of having learnt that hurting others would give me alleviation only intensified the bullying. To stand up for myself I would hurt others who were bullying me and they would hurt me even further in return. It was a never ending cycle. Therefore at age 32 when I learned that you have to treat anger and hatred with kindness I was alleviated of a maladaptive behavior that had been isolating me for years.

Finally, one of the most important takeaways that I've found out just recently is having mutuality with a bully. The same kids I went to middle school with are the same adults I still sometimes hang out with today. For years I would get anxiety before hanging out with them because I knew I would be at the bottom of the social stratum and have to deal with a lot of flak. I utilized the peer principle of mutuality to combat the power dynamics that had been created. Over the years these guys had a habit of thinking they were above me and would speak down to me and disparage me, sometimes jokingly and other times crossing the line. I was told in return that you are above them. When I attempted to assert power or superiority over the bullies they would always try to one up me. It became a damaging competition where everyone lost. When I sought to be on equal footing with bullies things changed. The bullies recognized mutuality and copied the behavior that had been bestowed upon them and became my friends. It's a natural human practice to treat others the way we are treated, whether it's for better or for worse. When I was mutual with the bullies they became mutual with me and we were on equal footing. We had a really good time the first night I tried this and I'm looking forward to spending time with them. The reason this works is because bullies have also been the victim of bullying. Therefore if you try to be superior to them they become afraid because when they were bullied there may have been emotional, verbal, or other types of abuse that are still lurking within their unconscious minds that they're afraid of and being at the bottom of this power dynamic immediately triggers these fears. Triggering these fears they jump into action and in their minds the only safe place is being at the top of the social

stratum and they'll do anything to get there regardless of your feelings. This ranges from making fun
of you to physical abuse at times too. Therefore
when you are mutual with them, their fears aren't
triggered, they copy your behavior, and you are
also not below them. There's social, mental, and
emotional safety for everyone.

Defense Mechanisms, Bullying, and Psychosis

During middle school I was picked on and bullied to the point of nearly committing suicide and all the friends I had from grammar school had completely turned on me. In the midst of this I developed a number of defense mechanisms that were subconscious and preventing me from socializing and connecting to people in positive ways. After joining a fraternity in college I developed schizophrenia and lost all my friends again. The treatment we were subjected to as pledges was dehumanizing and confounding in many ways and was one of the major causes of my psychosis. It was an eight month process of constant abuse which for reasons unknown to me at the time I decided to subject myself to. During this process I put up more defense mechanisms and I got to the point where I was completely socially dysfunctional. In these moments I felt there were a number of different things I could say, none of which seemed right, and it felt impossible to connect to others. Being in social situations was stressful and felt like a ton of work. The dichotomy was that within my conscious mind I wanted friends but within my subconscious mind I was pushing people away to maintain my safety, to stay alive, and to alleviate psychosis. From being suicidal in middle school I had learned people were dangerous, because their abuse made me suicidal. I had always felt like I was on a different wave length than everyone else and I didn't have a way of tapping into the common threads of socialization that everyone else seemed to so easily access. I had felt that if I didn't need to socialize with others I simply wouldn't. The irony I faced was that I needed people, but interacting with them was painful. This led me to realize I needed to learn and unlearn a lot more to unlock my psychosis.

As I disassembled the thought webs which comprised my psychosis I realized I had many un-intentional ways of pushing others away. My doctor and I talked about trust being an issue for me which it certainly was. Over the years I had adopted the behaviors of my bullies towards myself and some-times towards others as well. After unlearning these behaviors my psychosis partially lifted and I started feeling better about myself. I started seeing my life in a new way and for the first time in over twenty years I had positive and healthy self-esteem. After realizing I am a likable person and someone who is worth being friends with, I felt a sense of deservedness. The deservedness came from a feeling that I was a good person and also the feeling that other people were starting to like me. People would comment that I was a good person and they liked being around me but I would still push them away. There were many attempts by others to assure me that I was a good person which I really appreciated but there were misinterpretations of my behavior. I knew I was a good person when I was pushing them away but I wasn't even consciously aware I was doing things to push others away. In these moments I felt bad that I was pushing them away and I knew I was saying things that were hurtful and kept others at distance but I just didn't know why. During these moments the pushing of others away was where the negative emotions came from, and not necessarily from my overall evaluation of myself. These moments did make me feel like a bad person in some ways but the core issue was the defense mechanisms.

However, I finally had a breakthrough and realized I was subconsciously and unintentionally keeping distance from others as a means of protecting myself which had been a survival technique in middle school and the fraternity. I had many delusions regarding the innumerable ways I figured there would be another exodus of friendship and love within my life. I had to break down and refute all the ways in which I thought everyone would leave my life. The majority of these beliefs were irrational but I had to dig them out. I wrote in my journal that hatred, disparagement, making others hate me, and making others dislike me are not good defense mechanisms. I realized increasingly more that the defense mechanisms others used to keep me away during my episodes, when I was fairly socially awkward and abrasive, and during middle school, where I was just young and confused, were the exact things I was doing to keep other people away from me. I used a catch it, check it, change it journaling technique where I wrote in my journal not to use these abusive treatments as defense mechanisms and it helped incredibly. The underlying commonality in breaking down the defense mechanism was unlearning all the unhealthy and hurtful ways I was using to keep people away. I also had to realize there were instances I needed healthy defense mechanisms. A part of my learning curve was figuring out what these were and how to implement them in forgiving and kind ways.

On a metacognitive level I noticed my mental clarity immensely improved and my emotional health improved substantially. From an external perspective socialization was becoming more natural. I finally felt like I was on a similar wavelength as other people. I still had some trust issues and it was initially terrifying to take down my defense mechanisms. The fear came from feeling I would be hurt, and that all the things I was protecting myself from would happen. However, my fears never came to fruition. Being twenty years removed from middle school and ten years removed from the fraternity, I was getting different reactions to my behaviors. My behaviors were now positive and healthy and I was treating others well and this was a product of having unlearned the abusive socialization behaviors I had been practicing. This was also a product of taking many notes on how I wanted to treat people and on how to navigate social situations. Socialization never came easy for me even from a young age so learning how to socialize for me was a process of note taking, reflection, and writing, rather than just intrinsically knowing what to do and say. Combining this with unlearning my defense mechanisms I found I was finally connecting to people. It became incredibly easy to know what to say and do and it was an immense relief. I found when I wasn't pushing people away it was changing the way the interactions were going. The change in the interactions was fostering positive social interaction and for the first time since pledging the fraternity, socialization was an enjoyable experience. There was a shift in the way people reacted to me when I wasn't pushing them away along with finally knowing how to treat others well. This combination has changed my social life and I'm now usually busy three to four nights per week. The more important part of this is that I'm actually enjoying being around other people which was never the case beforehand. Removing this thought web has been an essential part in breaking down and eradicating my psychosis.

Competitive Thinking

Growing up I was always very competitive with my peers and in everything I did. I played sports and I constantly was taught that I had to be better than everyone else. Being in a capitalist culture there is a constant competitive drive for people to prove they are the best in order for their products or services to beat out their competition's which was also a way competitive thinking was impressed upon me. I had adopted these beliefs after hearing them throughout my life. In later years this carried over to my personal life and my life as a writer and it was detrimental to my overall well-being.

Having schizoaffective disorder did cause a lot of problems with socialization, but the thing I learned was that I had a lot of other socialization problems that were completely separate from the illness that may have contributed to symptoms. However once the cycle was initiated it was a circle of having symptoms which caused negative social interactions and then having those negative social interactions cause more symptoms. Difficulty socializing in the past six years after my second episode of schizoaffective disorder has caused me a lot of stress, and stress has been a trigger for a lot of symptoms. I realized that I had to start with the things I could control and the social trauma and negative interactions were things I could work with while the symptoms were things I just had to cope with. I think the important thing I realized is that all my life's traumas have factored into causing symptoms and difficulties and the way to find better mental health for me has been to address each trauma when the time was right for me to do so.

I realized throughout my life I had difficulty socializing because I was always trying to be better than others. In middle school I was picked on to the point of nearly committing suicide, so afterwards I had a strong inclination to establish superiority over those who bullied me and everyone else I met going forward. For me, this was a defense mechanism as I was afraid that I would be picked on again. It was subconscious but the behavior I learned was that I had to be superior to others as a means of survival, because when I wasn't it nearly lead to my death. Unlearning this behavior had a lot to do with unraveling competitive thinking. I first had to realize that working with people and not trying to be superior to them wasn't going to cause them to tell me to kill myself thus leading to suicide attempts. It actually had the opposite effect where people were more respectful that I was on equal footing and not putting myself above anyone which I'll talk about more soon.

Having schizoaffective disorder has meant being on a different timeline than everyone else. There were years where my friends were getting married, had great jobs, and were buying houses while I was living at home and not making very much money. This caused a ton of negative emotions and even depression for many years. Just recently I've been catching up on a few of these things but even after I bought a home, started improving my social life where I had regular friends again, and obtained a job as a peer specialist which I truly enjoy I still wasn't happy. I realized this was because I was constantly comparing myself to everyone else and I wasn't evaluating my happiness based upon how I felt. No matter how hard I worked or how successful I was at anything I still wasn't happy. I felt stress and anxiety and depression.

I made a paradigm shift realizing there will always be someone who has a better life and or a more difficult life than me but I can always just be a good person. I learned that life isn't about being better than others and proving that I was better than others. None of that matters at all. Life is about helping other people and working together to ensure that everyone can eventually find happiness and peace.

When I stopped comparing my life to other people's lives I realized that I truly do enjoy my life and I like being me. Getting rid of all my comparisons took a huge weight off my shoulders and allowed me to relax and stop worrying about improving for the sake of being better than others. I no longer had the burden of having to worry about who and or how many people were doing better than me and trying to catch up to them or surpass them. This lead to a wealth of happiness I previously felt I could not have had. Understanding that I was working with others instead of in competition with them allowed me to have a number of positive emotions and helped my social interactions immensely. Some of which were being happy instead of resentful towards all the people who were doing better than me financially, socially, and professionally. This transformed a number of negative thoughts and emotions into positive ones.

When I had originally been competing with others, without being aware of it, to be smarter than them or have more money or to just have a better life it was detrimental in my social interactions. When I had previously been competing with others they were working against me but when I decided to be on everyone's side I found I had more friends and supporters than I ever could have possibly imagined having. My willingness to help others created a willingness for them to help me. It was the key that unlocked some of my social inhibitions. People began to like me a lot more now that I was being a good friend and had their best interest in mind. I think previously I had people's best interest in mind but it was only if I was going to be better than them. I learned that mutuality in friendships is a key component to keeping good bonds and when I was previously a competitive person I wasn't able to maintain mutuality because of my desire to be better than others. Overall, I learned that it's the people in my life and the connections to my family and friends that are the true source of happiness and that all other achievements and success are good but were insufficient without the love of my family and friends.

Perfection; A False Standard

Being a perfectionist was something that was drilled into my mind from a very early age. Perfection was the ideal and anything short of it was seen as a failure. After my episodes I was very perfectionistic and this value really hampered my ability to function mentally and also within the world.

My perfectionism after my episodes was derived from a desire to control things that were beyond my control. For me, being in episodes of schizoaffective disorder was very precarious and I always felt like I had no control over anything, including my mind, which was a terrifying experience. To gain control I felt I had to be as perfect as possible to program my mind to do the right things if I ever lost control from psychosis again. After a while, I realized that this perfectionism was hampering me and preying upon me. Something I originally saw as a defense mechanism was actually a very serious behavioral pattern that was causing more psychosis. The amount of mental and behavioral rigidity that stemmed from this ideal had to be fought and eliminated.

When first combatting perfectionism, I was measuring success in black and white terms. I thought if things were perfect I was in the right and I was doing really well, but anything short of perfection was a failure and meant I was a failure. I also thought if I'm not striving for perfection than nothing else is worth striving for. After some reflection I realized that being human means to be imperfect. I learned that I don't have to strive for perfection to be a part of the group and it's incredibly unhealthy in a lot of ways to have an expectation of perfection. As a human being, it should be the expectation that we're all going to make mistakes and once I realized this it took a lot of pressure off me. I began to measure life in terms of progress and improvement within my work and I learned that I don't have to fully succeed in my goals to have gained success from an experience. Sometimes mistakes can be our greatest learning points, and the more I looked at mistakes as opportunities for growth the less salient it became to make them. Once I allowed myself to make mistakes and saw them as positive learning experiences my mental rigidity began to lift. Before I had changed my ideals I had no room for error and I thought terrible things would happen if I made mistakes, which hasn't been the case, but the experience of feeling a complete lack of control from episodes of psychosis had made me feel that way.

Another facet of having unlearned perfectionism was that my mood and self-esteem began to improve immensely. Marketing and societal ideals have a tendency to not allow us to feel good about ourselves if we're not perfect, which as humans we never can be. The impetus for perfection is buying a product or service that is supposed to but can never fulfill the in-satiety that the advertisements create. Once I unlearned that I don't need to be perfect I began taking it easier on myself. I started learning that I don't need perfection to feel good about myself and that I should not make perfection an expectation for anyone. It was incredibly uplifting emotionally when I changed my expectations from perfection to imperfection along with the disciplinary measurements that accompanied this. Being able to make mistakes also meant still being kind and compassionate towards myself and others when they happened as opposed to sternly disciplining myself and others. Having an allowance and understanding that mistakes are going to happen improved my social interactions immensely. When I allowed my friends to make mistakes and I just went with the flow and let them go, people wanted to be around me more and my friend circles grew.

Growing up in athletics, anything short of perfection was disciplined sternly, as well as from other sources too. Unlearning the harsh discipline that was instilled upon me and the fear that had been driven into my mind from coming short of perfection was really helpful. I realized I was being motivated by a fear of falling short of an ideal that as a human being I would never be able to attain. I was within a behavioral pattern that was designed to set me up for failure, discipline myself harshly, and then move me to action to try attaining that same unreachable goal of perfection again. I learned perfection is a false standard and it's not human. I also realized that in other areas of my life I need to stop setting myself up with expectations that are not reasonable and that once I fall short of, I'll sternly discipline myself for.

Mistakes are the essence of life, and they're a really good source of humor as well. Being in a world that doesn't measure success in all or nothing terms has been really helpful. It's allowed me to see even when I don't achieve the results I want from a situation that there are still small successes within those situations that can be cultivated and carried forward to the next opportunity. Seeing experiences in terms of having a mixture of good and bad as opposed to being entirely perfect or short of perfect, gave me a much more accurate picture of the world, and more accurate assessments of people in general. I no longer expected others to be perfect and this allowed me to accept their bad qualities along with their good, and to also do this for myself.

Stigma Doesn't Have to Hold You Back

Good Men Project, January 2018

Living with schizoaffective disorder for the past twelve years has been a precarious journey which has taught me a lot. When I was first diagnosed I was afraid of hearing the diagnosis and I was afraid of the stigma surrounding it. I didn't want to think that I was any different than anyone else. I soon learned that I had a lot of trauma I had to confront and neutralize however, along the way I realized I am just as human as everyone else.

Being someone who still has symptoms of schizophrenia and bipolar disorder who is very high functioning is a different position to be in. Most of the people in my life don't know about my diagnosis and I'm able to function well enough where I own a home, I have two jobs, I'm a writer, and I have a vibrant social life. However, while socializing with others there's a lot of stigma that gets thrown around which I can't necessarily speak out against at times. I usually only let the people closest to me know about my diagnosis because I understand they won't treat me differently for it. This is why I usually keep quiet when people use derogatory terms regarding people with mental health issues.

Saying something to stand up for myself in these situations usually indicates that I have a vested interest in mental health which can lead to some awkward questions for me. I tend to think it would lead to diagnosis disclosure which is not usually my goal.

I can only speak for myself but the times I get insulted and my feelings are hurt are when people single out those with mental health disorders. When someone says something like "he belongs in an asylum," or "he's a schizo" after someone is socially dysfunctional and/or acting awkwardly; that really hurts my feelings. This hasn't been said about me to my face but I usually hear it when people around me who don't know about my diagnosis are talking about others. I feel it in my heart and I can't say anything against it because I don't want people knowing about my diagnosis. I don't want people to exclude me from the group for having been hospitalized twice and for having a schizophrenia type diagnosis. It hurts because I didn't know how to solve the problems I was having with my mental health when I was having them. I didn't know how to solve my issues when I was hospitalized and I still have issues from schizoaffective disorder that I'm figuring out but I don't quite understand. These people who insulted me took their mental health for granted and estranged me from the group without knowing they were doing so. Without knowing it, they were basically saying the things I had been through made me a less rational and less healthy and less likable human being and I didn't belong with the rest of the group of people who could be deemed "healthy". There was an "us and them" and they were us and I was them and I felt excluded. The things I least liked about myself and didn't know how to change were keeping me separated from the way I wanted to be.

However, there are terms that are used that don't insult me too. There were also times where my friends who knew about the diagnosis were afraid to use certain words like crazy and psychotic. This was more immediately after my diagnosis but the thing they came to realize was that I also use the word crazy. I usually refrain from the word psychotic unless I'm describing a medical condition. I've found that euphemisms can be a good thing. Sometimes with language there are only so many ways to describe the way someone is acting or the way a situation is and people just blurt out these words, myself included. Having been through two psychotic episodes where I was nearly homeless, nearly starved to death, thought I was going to be the next messiah and save the world, and where I had auditory and visual hallucinations I don't take offense to these words and I don't do so intentionally.

Although there were times where it was painful to hear these words I've gotten healthy enough where I don't necessarily associate myself with words like crazy and/or psychotic. I realize there were times where I was very much crazy and/or psychotic throughout the day however, I can't live in a world where someone else's word use is restricted by my own experiences. My measuring stick for the use of words like these is basically if someone isn't intending to insult me for having a mental illness then I don't take their word choices such as psycho and crazy offensively. It seems ironic that someone with a mental illness wouldn't stand against such tactless word choice at times, however, it was alleviating for me to hear others speak to me the way they would normally speak to someone who doesn't have a mental illness. Using these words around me meant that they didn't consider me crazy and they didn't consider me psychotic. It meant they accepted me for who I am which is a rational and highly functioning individual.

Most importantly it meant that they weren't exclud-
ing me from the group by their word choice or de-
nouncing me as a lesser person for having a mental illness. It was the exact opposite where they
considered me so much a part of the group and
their friend that they could use these words without
insulting me because they knew that I knew how
much they cared for me. I almost felt not using
those words around me would be a form of exclud-
ing me because they wouldn't do that with anyone
else. I also wasn't wasting energy getting angry at
people when they had no intention of hurting my
feelings. With word choice some people were simply limited with language and had no other way of
describing what they had experienced or seen.

Allowing others to use these words around
me created an inclination to consider myself a
healthier person. If other people were doing crazy
things that I wasn't doing this meant that I was being rational. It proved to me that even though there
was a time I had been in a state of psychosis for
several years I was no longer in that time period.
Allowing myself to label some of my past actions as
crazy helped me to disassociate myself with my
past delusions and past traumas. Thinking I was
going to get a letter to Hogwarts (was true and I

laugh about it) but it was also considerably crazy, however, I no longer expect that letter therefore I'm a more rational human being. I now like to joke it's because of my age and not because of my magical ability.

I lecture about my experiences with schizoaffective disorder a lot and a commonality I've experienced is that people become tentative to ask me questions about the disorder. I always start by saying you can ask me anything and if I don't want to answer the question I'll just ask for the next question. Some people are still very tentative and I find this to be burdensome, not necessarily for me but more so for them. The reason I speak about intent with word choice is also because I speak about it with questions. If someone doesn't intend to hurt my feelings with a question I decide not to be offended by what they say. When I speak to people who are initially tentative to ask me questions I feel some of it is a self-consciousness that they'll say the wrong thing and be labeled as socially intolerant. This fear sometimes creates an overly self-conscious state of mind for some of these folks and they are so afraid to say the wrong thing that they don't say anything at all. Whenever someone asks a question that's a little over the line or could be considered offensive, I don't chide them or put them down. I simply answer the question to its truest intent. I don't want people to be afraid to use the wrong language when they're asking me questions to learn more about how to help people with my same disorder. I don't want people to become so overly self-conscious that they accidentally say things they normally would never say. For me, one of the best ways of helping stigma to be erased is by allowing people to stumble and spin their wheels with me and with questions they ask me until they realize they can ask me anything they want. I want them to feel comfortable talking about issues that aren't necessarily their own and not having to fear insulting me for using the wrong choice of words. I want the dialogue to be an open dialogue where we can address people's concerns and considerations openly and honestly and help them to learn. Schizoaffective disorder is a very difficult thing to understand if you haven't experienced it, therefore generating more open dialogue about it is the best way to quash stigma. If someone is afraid to ask me a question that they may feel is prejudiced, how will I ever get rid of their misinformation if I never know about it. It simply would never be addressed and it would dwell in a place that hampers that person in their interactions until it finally gets addressed or maybe never does.

I also want people to be able to hang out with me and use the exact same language they would as if they were with people who didn't have any diagnosis. To me, them using this type of language around me is more accepting of my condition and it's more true to the diagnosis. Sometimes it helps me to forget I even have a diagnosis which is something I enjoy doing frequently. There are times where I still have hallucinations and other symptoms however, it's not all the time. And having symptoms of schizoaffective disorder that can be labeled as crazy and/or psychotic doesn't mean that I am crazy and/or psychotic overall as a person. In fact it categorizes craziness and psychosis as a human condition that happens for all people, with or without a diagnosis because they use these words to describe all people and not just a particular group of people such as people who have psychotic disorders. The words simply describe a state of being during a particular moment in time, and they don't single me out in any way shape or form for having a diagnosis of schizoaffective disorder.

Mental Health and the Media: A Call to Action
Good Men Project, November. 2018

Having a diagnosis of schizoaffective disorder has been difficult because of the symptoms but also because of the stigma I've had to face. There have been many misconceptions about mental illness propagated by media sources like movies, the news, and television shows over the years. Whenever I used to turn on the news I would hear comments about how people who committed crimes had some sort of connection to mental illness. It's been statistically proven that people with diagnoses of mental illness are less likely to commit crimes than those who are just normal people. There were also many movies that stigmatized mental illness and shaped the way people thought about those who had a mental illness, creating misconceptions and prejudices surrounding those who had been diagnosed. For years it made it difficult for me to disclose my diagnosis because I wasn't certain of what others would think of me, or if they'd judge me or treat me differently. I still use critical discretion with whom I do and don't disclose my diagnosis.

However, at this critical point in history, there are those out there who are willing to challenge the misconceptions and prejudices of stigma.

In recent years the media has begun making a point of prioritizing mental health issues as being valid and commonplace. It's been inspiring to hear stories of professional athletes, tv personalities, and actors who have battled mental illness to lead successful lives. There are currently a number of diagnoses that have been labeled as acceptable to be living with and still some that have yet to be broached; pop culture singer Adele has spoken out about depression, Brandon Marshal has been living with borderline personality disorder, Delante West manages bipolar disorder, and Lady Gaga has been working through anxiety. There also was recently an anti-bullying campaign put on by The New York Yankees to help a local fan who had been bullied by his peers. All these achievements in social justice have been wonderful to watch and it's been really helpful for me to see mental illness being humanized, as it should be. One of the latest achievements Hollywood has made in humanizing mental illness has been Silver Linings Playbook. Another movie that made a good effort but fell short was A Beautiful Mind.

A Beautiful Mind is a story about John Nash who was a Pulitzer prize winner in economics for creating Game Theory which is an economic system used to analyze and dictate behavioral relations. However, being someone with schizophrenia and seeing how misrepresented John Nash was in the movie was somewhat disturbing. I think one of the last frontiers of mental illnesses to be broached are psychotic disorders. In the movie John Nash is portrayed as speaking with an individual who follows him around on his daily routine. Having been someone who has had hallucinations I know what it's like to have voices separate from my own speaking to me, but they are a breach of the unconscious mind and don't take the form of someone walking beside me. I've also had visual hallucinations but for visual and auditory hallucinations to combine into the shape of a person separately speaking to someone outside of themselves is almost unheard of. In psychology, it's almost a direct indication to malingering symptoms or falsely reported symptoms for clinical staff if someone reports seeing and talking to someone as if they are a fully visible and speaking person in the room. To further this point, with many other movies I've noticed movie companies have taken full advantage of the buzz surrounding the word psychosis, and psychotic disorders.

Being someone who works in an in-patient and out-patient setting and having lived with psychosis for twelve years, it's safe to say psychotic disorders have been completely misrepresented and stigmatized by the media and by popular culture. For myself, and most of the people whom I work with on in-patient and out-patient settings they are normal people who live full lives. They have great senses of humor and have high levels of integrity, and are really enjoyable to spend time with. These people are intelligent, have families and are very caring and conscientious people. While interacting with them, you would not know they had a psychotic disorder unless they specifically told you so. People with psychotic disorders are not screaming and in chains and locked up and hurting people the way they have been portrayed in movies. They are REAL people whom you interact with on a daily basis without knowing so. About 1 percent of the population has schizophrenia meaning, 1 in 100 people you interact with on a daily basis has schizophrenia which is one of the most commonly known psychotic disorders. Before I had schizophrenia there was never a time during the day and even now there isn't unless I'm at work where I have thought, *"this person definitely has schizophrenia, I'm certain of it, I know what it looks like and I know how people with schizophrenia are."* This in fact probably has never happened for most people because there haven't been any movies portraying how people with schizophrenia truly are and truly interact with others. This doesn't happen because movies can't depict what people with schizophrenia look like simply because they would have to put ordinary people on the screen doing and saying ordinary things.

My current standing is that I'm grateful to the media for the progress it has helped create in humanizing some mental health disorders, but the next step forward is humanizing psychotic disorders. Having a psychotic disorder in America is like living in the closet, you never want anyone to know because you're afraid of the repercussions. My call to action for the media is to take the next step and humanize psychotic disorders until people are able to see me and everyone else for who they are, and not for an artificially applied label that misrepresents everything we stand for and are as people.

Symptoms and Solutions

Tools that have Helped Me to Face the Uncertainty of Mental Illness

Good Men Project, January 2019

Having uncertainty has been one of the most difficult and fearful parts of having schizoaffective disorder. There have been many times where I wasn't certain how my life would turn out or whether I would ever recover from the illness. Wrestling with uncertainty has been an adversity in itself.

When first diagnosed with schizophrenia and bipolar disorder simultaneously, I honestly didn't know what to think. I had a lot of misinformation about the illness from popular culture which made the diagnosis somewhat terrifying. However, as I acquired more knowledge about what I was really going through, it became easier to deal with the illness.

I think the first part to finding some peace with my diagnosis was knowing from experience what having schizophrenia meant and also knowing that people do recover from the illness on a regular basis. One of the most difficult parts about initially getting diagnosed was not knowing exactly what had been going on in my mind and what was causing me to be so dysfunctional mentally and emotionally. Learning that my symptoms were manifestations of trauma from earlier years in my life helped give me an understanding that I just had to work on my trauma to recover. I realized that as I continue to educate myself on schizoaffective disorder, the fear that came from not knowing what it was or how to deal with it began to dissipate. For me, education has been a useful combatant in dealing with uncertainty. Education has given me more control over my illness.

Going forward, I at least had an idea of how to improve my mental health. However, I still had the fear that I would not have a full life. There were years I spent working hard on my mental health, day in and day out, and the part of not knowing whether my life would turn out for the better was very painful. I felt like my suffering had no ending because there was no paradigm for when I would recover. There wasn't a set date that my life would change and there weren't days I could leave the house without my coat of schizophrenia and bipolar disorder. Not knowing at which point I would be back to myself and free of pain was agonizing. Not knowing when or if my life would ever get to a place I wanted it to be caused a lot of hopelessness. Along with this, the hopelessness caused a lot of fear and negative emotions. When I felt uncertain of whether I could have the life I wanted, it was very difficult to work towards creating that life.

However, as I began making breakthroughs that improved my mental health I started realizing that I maybe could one day recover. I started believing in myself because I was proving that I could make progress and improve my mental health through hard work. Turning uncertainty into certainty helped change my hopelessness to hope. During some of the darker years of my life, hope was derived from the belief or partial certainty that I would one day overcome all the adversity I had been going through. I would one day live a life where I didn't wander through the day constantly dealing with emotional and mental pain from my trauma. I began to believe in myself and believing in myself was a manifestation of having some sort of certainty that my efforts would not be fruitless. This certainty was derived from taking more longitudinal looks at my life. I would look back six months to a year and make assessments realizing my health and life were better than they had been. My efforts and my belief in myself were the fuel that motivated me to continue to work and progress through some of my darkest hours.

Sometimes just the fear of facing uncertainty on smaller scales was difficult. For example, I had a fear that I would get made fun of by other people and I was terrified of it. My doctor asked me "What would happen if they made fun of you?" I answered, "it would be embarrassing. He asked, "What would happen after that?" And I replied, "I wouldn't know what to say." He asked, "What would happen after that?" And I said, "They would laugh at me." He asked, "What about after that?" And I answered, "I would go make new friends." This process of taking my uncertainty and exploring all possible outcomes to the greatest extent by asking questions has been a useful practice for me. I found many times I was afraid to ask myself what would happen because I was so afraid to face the uncertainty.

I also found that when I thought out what would happen with my uncertainties, even in the worst case scenarios, I had nothing to fear. I was more afraid of uncertainty in my life than I was with knowing what the worst case scenarios could be. So knowing the worst case scenarios became a reprieve for me and I learned for me that even having a certainty as to what the worst possible outcome could be was less fear provoking than simply not knowing.

While working through these difficult years I realized that finding certainties in uncertain times created hope and motivation to continue forward. Although my social life was in disrepair and my mental functionality was not where I wanted it to be, I still had some certainties. One of them was that my parents were always going to keep a roof over my head. Knowing I had food and shelter was very comforting as I had nearly starved to death in my first episode. Knowing that visiting my doctor helped improve my mental health every week also provided some hope. Knowing my Dad would take me golfing and my family was never going to leave me was also very comforting.

I think above all though, having made progress was one of the biggest motivators that fueled my recovery. After developing the ability to effectively alleviate mental health burdens I had some certainty that I wasn't fighting a losing battle. I knew that I had the tools I needed to combat schizoaffective disorder.

My recovery tools

Being a good person, making as many good decisions in my life overall as I could, going to therapy, journaling, reading good literature and acquiring as much wisdom as possible, and making certain I was treating people well.

I found that when I did these things, I developed the realization that I was more successful and better able to cope with my illness. Having a plan that worked in combatting my mental illness fueled the fire and motivated me to work harder than ever to get rid of the ailment. Developing my tools in journaling and talk therapy came in the form of self-educating and asking for psychological education from my doctor. There still were times periodically where I felt hopeless and during these times I did have suicidal thoughts.

After seven years of periodically having suicidal thoughts I came to realize that I usually felt suicidal when I felt stuck. Feeling stuck meant I had problems I felt I couldn't fix and I had no belief in myself whatsoever that I would be able to fix them. The most important tool that has helped me during these times is knowing that I've been in these times before and I've been successful in finding the necessary wisdom to pacify the burdens of trauma. Having faith in myself has and will continue to be the certainty I need to give me hope to fight through some of the darkest moments of my life. I never started out with the requisite tools and resources to overcome mental illness, but through hard work and being a good person, I developed them and I'm certain that everyone else can too.

Letting Go of Control

My episodes of schizoaffective disorder were a very precarious time where everything felt out of control. I had a number of symptoms that were beyond my comprehension and I started trying to control everything in my life in order to minimize my symptoms. This desire to control everything and everyone led to a lot of difficulty in a number of ways for me in later years.

The first thing I struggled with was trying to control other people. During episodes I had a number of situations where people were harmful towards me so I feared if I wasn't able to control them there would be serious repercussions. In later years I learned to live along the lines of "live and let live" in a variety of ways. The first things I wrote down were that I am not responsible for what everyone thinks and feels and it's not my job to regulate their thoughts and emotions. I also wrote that I don't have to do this in order to save the world or be a messiah. During my episodes I used to think that my thoughts were being broadcasted on a telepathic network. In later years I knew none of this was true but the thoughts still lingered. Proving this wrong is seemingly obvious and fruitless but I've found for myself until I refute delusions within my journal they have a tendency to affect my life in subtle ways. This process of refuting delusions in my journal helped improve my mental and emotional health. My mental clarity improved and I felt my emotional burdened lightened with each delusion I refuted. The thing I found conversationally when allowing others to think and feel what they wanted to, was that they allowed me to do the same. People tend to mimic the behavior that is directed towards them within social constructs. The irony was that I originally thought controlling others would give me freedom from them. However, not controlling them liberated me from others trying to be controlling of me. This wasn't always the case but even when others were trying to be controlling I learned that I didn't feel compelled to follow their orders because that wasn't the way that I treated other people. When I direct a behavior towards other people I tend to feel deserving of that same behavior, however when I do not direct a behavior towards others I do not feel responsible to put up with that same behavior when it's brought in my direction. I had an expectation to receive the same treatment I was providing and this was liberating because it became much easier to disagree with

92

others and to be independent when I needed to. I felt less compelled to do what others wanted me to and to just follow my heart with my mind.

The only catch was that I worried that I had to prevent other people from making mistakes. I learned that it varies based upon the consequences of the action. If the consequences are smaller, I found it's sometimes better to allow others to make mistakes instead of correcting them. Making mistakes can be good teaching points for others and they appreciate the allowance for their autonomy. In immediate years after my episodes I found with family interactions I preferred for family members to allow me to make mistakes as opposed to regulating every little nuance of my life. I didn't care that I made mistakes and had to fix them. I had felt so over-regulated growing up that I had never developed the tools and resources to live independently. The immediate several years after my second episode were developmental for me and I felt I had to do things for myself to learn how to do them. This was my main style of learning. I had been previously angry at my parents for trying to tell me everything to do and say while growing up which was the reason I had stopped talking to them during my episodes. I felt their over-baring nature, or at least the perception thereof, had stripped me of my independence and that I wasn't prepared to live independently when I was finally allowed out of their grasp of high school years and living with friends in college.

Another important facet of control was realizing how much was or wasn't within my control. Immediately after my episodes I was trying to control people and situations that simply weren't within my control or my purview. People tend to get angry and push you away when you are asserting yourself in their lives when you are not being asked to do so and also when it's not your place. This was somewhat isolating. I had to learn to allow people to screw up and only to step in if I saw serious consequences developing. The other part about trying to control things that were out of my control was that it wasted a tremendous amount of emotional and cognitive resources. I would get frustrated that I couldn't control other people in social situations and I felt controlling others would help me to have friends.

I realized that I had to "change myself, and I would change my world" (Ghandi). In the first couple years out of my episodes I had a great deal of social ineptitude but I wasn't willing to blame myself

94

for it. I allocated blame to others but eventually realized that I was the common denominator in all my
social situations that weren't going well. This was a
difficult thing to tell myself but it was an important
truth to bare. It made me realize that all I had to do
was develop my social and interpersonal skills to
have the social life I wanted. I started taking a lot of
notes after every social interaction on what went
well and what could be improved and how to improve it. I took notes on what to say and not to say
in social situations. What helped me was that knowing the rules of a social situation gave me control
over it. Knowing the rules helped me to realize
when I couldn't and couldn't break them and/or had
to break them. Realizing that the only person I was
really able to change was myself liberated me from
my social ineptitude and helped me develop friendships again. I found I was still putting forth the
same effort in terms of emotional and cognitive resources but the benefits were compounding because I was focusing my efforts towards myself
which was something I had responsibility over and
also control over. Focusing my efforts towards
things I could change (attributes of myself) allowed
me to develop the requisite tools and resources to
have the social life that I wanted. As I became in-

creasingly healthier I learned that I had been the one that needed to change and that it wasn't everyone else.

Treating Mania as an Addiction
Good Men Project, June 2019

Having schizoaffective disorder bipolar type
for me, means having schizophrenia and bipolar
disorder. One of the most difficult parts of having
this disorder was the fact that I overlooked the bipolar facet of what I was going through. For years I
worked on limiting the schizophrenia symptoms and
dealing with them directly but I recently learned that
my bipolar symptoms and schizophrenia symptoms
have been amplifying one another. Therefore I have
made a more concerted effort to work on reducing
and limiting mania as well and working on the illness from multiple angles and not just focusing on
the psychotic features.

When I have been struggling with symptoms
of schizophrenia it has had a strong impact on my
mood making my life very emotionally difficult. In
psychosis it's similar to having a stuffy nose where
your mind feels bogged down and muddled and it
feels difficult to think and communicate the same
way your nose would feel when congested if you
were trying to breathe. This caused some major
depressive symptoms because I wanted to think
and function like everyone else and I felt my psy-

chosis was the reason I was unable to have some of the things I wanted in life at times. Also, I directly related some of my social inhibitions and inabilities to connect with people as being directly caused by psychosis thus triggering negative emotions. When I had these negative emotions it increased my stress levels because I put a lot of pressure on myself to get healthier in order to have a fuller life and a happy life. This added stress would cause hallucinations and added psychosis and an inability to think clearly. Having more stress has always directly correlated to an increase and/or amplification of my symptoms and less stress has done the latter.

After this happened I would be strongly motivated to work on my mental health which happened in the form of journaling and writing. I had a delusion for a while that I had to write to improve my mental health but also that I had to write in order to cause mania for myself. Mania can be difficult because it's a constant adrenaline rush throughout the entire day. It pulses through your thyroid gland and into your heart and your jugular vein and it is constant euphoria but also has a tinge of anxiety along with it. It was a very addicting feeling and I remember thinking during an episode," If everyone could feel this way they would never do drugs". I used to work twelve hour days on my feet while feeling mania without needing more than a half hour break day after days for five to six days a week every week going non-stop. During an episode I went 36 straight hours working without sleep while on a mania trip between schoolwork, class, and my job.

For years I had an unconscious thought from my episodes that I wanted to cause mania for myself and others. I had to search back during times in my episodes to realize that one of the origins of my mania was a result of wanting to become a writer. Making this realization helped me to neutralize the thought that I needed to cause mania for myself and or everyone through writing because it felt so good. There were also other delusions that were causing me to perpetuate my mania and addressing these thoughts one by one and making them into zeros started reducing the mania. I originally thought I needed the mania because it felt so good and I was afraid of depression because in middle school I had nearly committed suicide because of depression. I established that I wasn't going to commit suicide and be extremely depressed without having mania which took time.

I also realized that getting rid of mania helped me to be more stable mood wise and this clarified my thinking a great deal. I had learned that mania contributes to psychosis and my theory on this was that a constant stream of adrenaline rushing to my mind was causing me to think dysfunctionally. I also think that when I was addicted to mania I was thinking and saying things that would perpetuate my mania which was also problematic in my thought process and contributed to more psychosis. I had one thought in particular that I had to do anything and everything to the absolute best of my ability to be a writer and also to have mania. During episodes when I was doing this it was my main trigger for mania and the genesis of a lot of obsessive behaviors like washing my hands excessively to the point of them having tons of tiny little cuts and looking like they had been moved through buckets of glass.

This extreme perfectionist coupled with a fear of not having the addictive adrenaline rush of mania created a great deal of mental rigidity in social situations because I thought everyone and everything had to be perfect otherwise I wouldn't have this feeling and I might commit suicide without having mania. Therefore in social situations I was very unaccepting of other people's mistakes and I was way overly disciplined in what I allowed myself to say and also in how careful I was with every little thing I said and did. This self hyper-vigilance in social situations bogged me down immensely and made it nearly impossible to have a cordial conversation with others because I was constantly trying to correct them and also trying to be as perfect as I could with everything I said and did. This perfectionism caused by mania also contributed to my stress levels, increasing and causing hallucinations and other psychotic symptoms that were very difficult to navigate while simultaneously trying to hold a good conversation with someone.

Organization's Effects with Schizoaffective Disorder
Schizophrenia Bulletin by Oxford Medical Journals,
February 2018

Throughout my episodes of schizoaffective disorder and even afterwards I have had an obsession with organization. During my first episode, I heard a professor speaking of a writer as "an organizational genius." The idea really resonated with me. I started looking at the various ways that people organize their possessions. For instance, things might be arranged alphabetically or numerically. I finally settled on utility as an organizing principle. I wanted everything I owned to be organized in ways that would save me time, or make things easier to find, or create space. Although it may have been a good idea to get organized, I did it for all the wrong reasons.

Having often been ridiculed in grade school and in high school for my supposed lack of intelligence, I felt the need to show signs of my intelligence whenever possible. My being made fun of was very salient for me as it nearly led to suicide in seventh grade so I also had a strong subconscious motivation to want people to see me as intelligent. I felt that being organize would be a sign of intelligence to anyone who met me. This gave me hope that people would be more respectful of my intellectual abilities

Having schizoaffective disorder was a very precarious situation. My mind was scattered in a million places and my thoughts were constantly racing. I struggled to find the slightest bit of regularity and/or dependability upon my surroundings. Having the symptom of racing thoughts is similar to watching an old film reel being clipped by quickly. It's difficult trying to piece together everything happening and make sense of it. I thought if I could keep things organized externally then that would create internal organization. Also, I thought it would help clear up racing thoughts. Schizophrenia makes it difficult to discern between what is internal and what is external. Putting everything in its proper place was an attempt to clear my mind.

Organization gave me a sense of comfort and security; I could come home to my apartment and know exactly where everything was. I felt control over the possessions I owned, which gave me a sense of control over my life, something I completely lacked.

I once heard an existentialist quote which said, "There's no guarantee that everything is going to be in the same place where it previously was" I believed in this quote to a T and thought things weren't going to be in the same place all the time. Even the things I thought were the most stable and unchanging felt as if they had changed. The sense of control that organization gave me was pacifying but it is possible that part of the calming effect was not having to interact with other while I was at my apartment. Most of the emotional difficulties brought on by schizoaffective disorder came when I was interacting with other people. Though it felt as though the organization inside my apartment created a sense of safety, it may really have been just the fact that I was isolated and I did not have to deal with the adversity of social interactions while I was there.

Still I felt that if I could resolve the problem of organizing my possessions it would leave me one less problems to face. I felt that having found suitable places for all my possessions would clear space in my mind to think about and resolve other, more important issues. My mind felt like a crowded space at the time because of all the sleeplessness and other symptoms I was experiencing. I felt if I had more space in my apartment it would create more space in my mind and my mind would be able to function better.

Despite the false expectations I brought to the task, practicing organization critical thinking skills was a way learning useful concepts in a low stakes environment. The practice of organizing and bringing "chaos to order instead of an order to chaos" (Vonnegut) provided guidance for my thoughts and actions, but getting things organized didn't necessarily organize my mind. Organizing my mind in a better way was more a result of practicing prioritization, which is the organization of events. It was that constant practice of thinking about what I was doing which was most helpful for my cognitive development.

When things were disorganized I used to always feel that I had to organize them, but that's not necessarily the case anymore. My mind's functionality and clarity isn't dependent upon how well my possessions are organized externally. Using critical prioritization skills to make life easier is a practice that has helped improve the way I think, which has little to do with whether everything I own is in the "right" place.

My Experience with Hallucinations

Schizophrenia Bulletin by Oxford Medical Journals, October 2018

During my first two episodes of schizoaffective disorder I had very few hallucinations. It was only later that I had auditory, visual, and tactile hallucinations. Experience has shown me that the frequency of my hallucinations is directly related to my level of stress. In periods of low stress, I usually haven't experienced many. When my stress level has been higher I've had more.

The first hallucination I ever had was auditory. I was sitting alone at my parents house at age 25 after my second episode of schizoaffective disorder. My parents had left the house to go get dinner at a place that was forty five minutes away. The TV, radio, and anything that could make sound were turned off. I heard my mother's voice calling from the garage door. It said "Hey," and I looked in the direction the voice came from. After I realized no one was there and nothing that could produce sound was there I became concerned. I walked over and opened the garage door; my parents' car was gone.

That was an auditory hallucination that I label as repetitive. It was simply an echoing of something I had previously heard. Over time, I've learned to identify hallucinations like these but every time I hear them I still look in the direction that the sound came from. These repetitive hallucinations continue to happen periodically and I still look in the direction that they come from to realize no one is there. People ask if these are scary. I would say that these experiences are disconcerting, but they don't stress me out all that much. I know I can't do anything about them; since they are only repetitions of things I've heard before, there is nothing to fear. These I can feel in my frontal lobe, and they don't cause me any physical pain.

The other type of auditory hallucination that I've experienced for brief moments have been the kind I call a creative auditory hallucinations. That is when there has been an actual voice that's not my own creatively speaking to me. The only time I've had trouble with creative auditory hallucinations has been when I've been doing some heavy work in my journal coming to grips with past traumas. When journaling I sometimes crossed a thought that caused my brain to become dysfunctional. Sometimes, this has caused these creative auditory hallucinations. When this has happened I felt pain in the center of the top of my head. At first it was pretty terrifying to hear a voice that was not my own speaking to me but I've learned to neutralize the thoughts that triggered the creative auditory hallucinations which makes them go away. I guess my advice to anyone experiencing these types of hallucinations would be that your brain has not been occupied by another being. I believe that this kind of auditory hallucination is a voice from my unconscious mind surfacing to the conscious level. The unconscious mind is always at work and I think this is one of the ways it sometimes malfunctions with people who have schizophrenia.

I have also experienced visual hallucinations. My visual hallucinations have only been of the repetitive kind; I have only ever seen glimpses of things that I've seen in the past. The only type of visual hallucination I've ever had has been of people who are not actually there. When stressed, I've had glimpses of someone turning a corner. When I walk over to look around the corner no one is ever there. One trigger for these repetitive visual hallucinations is when something takes the shape of a human being. For example at my workplace we had a display of four boxes stacked like a podium with turnips on top. Every time I walked by it I had the hallucination of a person taking place in front of what could have been considered the shape of a bust of someone. The other thing I've noticed is that the color red seems to trigger these visual hallucinations more so than any other color. There have been many times where I have seen a red apron or red shirt and I have had a brief visual hallucination of a person in place of it. I sometimes wonder if red is a trigger because it's a primary color or it triggers some part of my mind that may be related to the hallucination. I'm uncertain if red is a color related to stress for me this meaning that when I see red it causes me stress thus triggering the hallucination. Thankfully, these hallucinations have only been very brief and have had very little effect on the way I live.

I have also experienced tactile hallucinations, dealing with the sense of touch. There have been times when it felt like a mosquito or spider was crawling on my leg and I looked down to get rid of it and nothing was there. These are also stress related hallucinations. These have been few and far between and also have not had much effect on my day to day activities. Fortunately, these sensations have always felt external so I simply check to see if anything is there and if not, I disregard it. This is an actual type of hallucination and it's not the same as feeling itchy. It feels as though something is actually crawling on or up my leg.

Over the years, I've realized because of social trauma from my past that some of the most stressful situations for me are when I'm with and around people. Generally places where I have been forced to socialize like work, parties, and large social gatherings have been the most stressful places for me causing more hallucinations. It's been important for me to be aware of which situations are stressful because this has given me a sense of when I may have hallucinations. This helps me to be prepared for those hallucinations and to have the expectation that if the hallucinations and stress are too much that I'll need to take a few minutes away from people, whether it be a break at work or just a few minutes not participating in a conversation at a party or while with others.

Elements of Thought Broadcasting

Good Men Project, February 2020

Feeling like my thoughts were being broadcasted to the world was a really difficult symptom to deal with during and after my episodes of schizoaffective disorder. Before my second hospitalization, I somehow believed stepping foot outside of a car would cause a nuclear holocaust due to thought broadcasting. Having the weight of such immense repercussions due to the actions of simply thinking and feeling thoughts and emotions caused a ton of psychosis. It was also really crippling mentally and emotionally and created a ton of fear and hyper-scrupulosity as I thought everything I did, said, thought, and felt would have tremendous repercussions. The fears this created were restricting in many ways.

The psychosis from the belief in thought-broadcasting came from several sources. During my episodes, I thought I had to save the world by learning good values and morals and by becoming a really good person. I thought that everything I was thinking and feeling was being disseminated to the entire world. I think a part of this belief had to do with having a mental awakening during my episode. Having awareness that people were reacting to me due to autonomous decisions made me feel I had agency over my life and unfortunately over the entire world. A part of adopting this belief was that I was only sleeping two to three hours per night and my mind wasn't functioning normally. Even in later years I knew these things weren't true but I had never really refuted them on paper. Pining through these thoughts and refuting them helped to alleviate their residual burden, as they still existed within my unconscious mind. I eventually refuted these delusions realizing I don't have control over the world and I don't want control over the world and this was a relief. Realizing I wasn't a messiah also made me realize even if everyone could hear my thoughts and emotions, no one was out to get me. Thinking I was a messiah had given me a great deal of paranoia in years past because of the thought that if there are people for me there must be people against me. However, when I realized if for the past eight years if someone has been out to get me, and they still haven't, this must mean I'm relatively safe.

Another part of this was being afraid people would think I was a strange person due to all the strange thoughts I had been having. This caused me initially to repress thoughts and emotions that were normal to have as a part of my brain's regular functioning. This repression caused phenomenology such as seeing visions of people, having my mind fog up, and getting ice pick type headaches in random parts of my brain. Initially after my second episode, I talked to my therapist and I realized strange thoughts are a normal thing for everyone to have. In later years I realized that if everyone was hearing everything I was thinking and feeling they obviously didn't care about what was happening inside my mind, and the world was exactly the same even if all these strange thoughts and emotions were being broadcasted. It also told me that no one was treating me any differently even if they could perceive everything going on inside my brain. This was an immense relief and helped to dispel the delusion. I know it sounds irrational but proving this delusion false on this level helped improve my mental functionality a great deal.

I also used to think if I was broadcasting thoughts it was my responsibility to make sure the world was getting good information to create a golden age and to save everyone and this practice made me a messiah. I also realized I had been having a number of different thoughts, ideas, and emotions some of which were good and others of which were bad, and the world had remained exactly the same. Nothing I was thinking or feeling had any influence on the way the world was functioning, operating, and on any global events what-soever. The news reports, newspapers, and other media outlets still had the same types of melancholy stories despite my efforts to constantly think good thoughts and to have the right meaning assigned to each and every thought and emotion. Realizing this helped me to let go of having to assign the correct meaning to each and every thought realizing it was fruitless to do so in terms of my delusions of trying to save the world. This also alleviated psychosis for me.

I think another part of this had to do with the mania involved as well. Mania provides an intense and almost euphoric and constant adrenaline rush, so it was addicting in some ways. This happened in direct correlation to me doing, thinking, saying, and feeling things I thought were all correct. This delusion also led me to believe I was a messiah as I thought I must be feeling this manic feeling for a reason. When I was willing to let go of the mania telling myself that I'm not a messiah and I'm not in control of the world, this helped clarify my thinking immensely. I started thinking more rationally and seeing things more clearly. Letting go of the mania for better emotional composure was a tremendous relief and the placidness of not feeling I was a messiah has felt a lot better than the adrenaline of thinking I was saving the world somehow.

Insights into Referential Thinking
Good Men Project, March 2020

Referential thinking to me is the idea that everything everyone was saying or doing was in direct relation to me. With psychosis, there was a process and a way of thinking that was ego-centric, and it really felt like I was getting secret messages from TV, the radio, professors at school, and everyone around me even when they weren't directly talking to me. Some of this line of thinking started with the mentality of "everything happens for a reason". From having watched years of television, where everything does happen for a reason and everything on the screen is interconnected in at least subliminal ways if not obvious ways, I developed this pattern of thinking. I think another facet of this also was the constant fear I had from living in the fraternity. Interpersonally I was struggling because of psychosis and everyone in the frat seemed to be against me, wanting to fight me, or wanting to hurt me. This created a hyper-vigilance coupled with thinking patterns that comprised referential thinking. Being constantly afraid caused me to constantly look for warning signs as to what might happen next and the fear of the fraternity members also threw off my thinking. During my episodes I was constantly looking for connections between things, even if they weren't connected, and this was a part of referential thinking. It was a defense mechanism to try to anticipate whether there would be problems thrown my way. I believe there were other factors as well but these seem to be the main events I can trace back as the root of the issue, as I believe most psychosis for me is rooted in life experiences.

As my mental health worsened over time, I lost faith in my own ability to listen to what I was thinking and my own logical reasoning and this led me to look outside of myself for guidance on what to say and do within every moment of the day. This led me to buying three hundred dollars in produce because I thought people were giving me signals to pick up the same foods they were. In retrospect, I was in a state of psychosis and these people could see to some extent I was not well. They might have looked at me worriedly, put produce in their carts, and then looked again because they were afraid of me. I couldn't see that when it was happening. Another contributing factor to looking outside of myself for guidance was having lost my ego-boundary. The ego-boundary is what separates the internal from the external world, telling you that these words on the page are outside of your mind while the thoughts within your head are inside your mind. When I lost my ego-boundary it felt like everything was just within one blend so it felt like external words and suggestions had internal standing and were happening in direct relation to my thoughts. Thinking this was happening contributed to me listening to people around me for guidance. I would think,"Should I buy strawberries." Someone would see me looking at the strawberries, pick up their own strawberries, look at me to walk past me, and then I interpreted this look as a suggestion that I should buy them.

Moving forward after my episodes, taking medicine was the first step to normalizing my mind. The medicine helped clear up my thinking and re-establish an ego-boundary to an extent but there was more work to be done. I had to unlearn the ways of thinking that anything and everything happening was related to me. A part of this was journaling that not anything and everything happens for a reason in real life. In fiction, anything within the art has a purpose and the same tends to go for commercials and even live television productions but in real life that's not true. Knowing that this is the nature of fiction and that real life is different helped me to start seeing how things were not connected. I strove to see how things were not connected and this was really helpful for me. The more I could see how things were disconnected the easier life became.

An important realization I made was to understand that no one from the fraternity is out to get me anymore. It took time to realize this as I wasn't fully rational after my episodes. Having run into a number of guys from the frat and seeing that they were happy to see me in later years helped me to realize that no one really cared anymore about how much I had been struggling interpersonally during those times. No one was mad at me or out to get me. Realizing this helped me to unlearn the defense mechanism of searching for clues and insights into reasons I'd need to defend myself. No longer having a reason to defend myself took down my guard which was really helpful.

Another realization that helped me was learning that the internal world does not have to be the same as the external world. During my episodes I had developed a belief and ideal that everything within my mind would be the same as everything I said externally. I wanted to be as genuine as possible, not realizing I was taking this to an unhealthy level. When I learned there are internal processes and thought patterns we all have that we don't express externally this was helpful. I had to learn that everyone has a different internal life and that our external lives are also different. I used to define myself and who I was in terms of what I was thinking and feeling. Moving away from this and defining myself by what I was saying and doing helped. Having space to think and feel whatever I wanted also alleviated a lot of symptoms. It helped me to realize I am a good person when for years I struggled to see that because I was judging myself based upon what I was thinking and feeling as opposed to what I was saying and doing.

Lastly realizing that I am not the center of the world was really helpful. I had been very egocentric during and after my episodes and getting rid of this behavior was really helpful. In fiction, most things happening have some relation to the main character or others characters. Even innocuous things such as people placing down a tea cup can have metaphoric standing and relation to the main character. When I finally realized most things people are saying and doing are not related to me, I was able to even further disconnect life and to see more clearly. Most of the things people were saying and doing had more to do with who they were than with me. I also realized that I might be at the center of my own world, but I'm not at the center of the entire world really helped. We are all at the center of our own worlds but within the world there is no real center. The world is a globe. This helped me learn that I'm a person amongst persons and even if things are happening around me they don't necessarily have relation to me or to what I'm thinking and feeling.

Psychosis; A Communication Disorder

During a dialogic training, Mary Olson mentioned the proposition of psychosis being a communication disorder, and this really resonated with me. Over the years I've found most of the work I've been doing has been a matter of establishing better communication within my mind so I could also do so interpersonally. Putting the onus on internal communication has been a really important guide to understanding how to combat and eliminate psychosis.

For several years I wondered whether I had Asperger's syndrome because socialization was incredibly difficult for me. I thought there was something biologically happening within my mind that had inhibited me socially for so many years. Knowing what to say or do in social situations seemed nearly impossible pretty much all the time. As I unraveled my psychosis I began to figure out how to socialize again. Over the years I've noticed how psychosis had a way of inhibiting my linguistic abilities within conversations but as the psychosis has lifted I've learned that I did not have any biological ailments contributing to my inability to socialize. As a kid I had a cognitive impairment but with medication I was commensurate socially to everyone around me. Without it, I struggled at times. However, after my episodes I struggled socially even while having medication. So a part of my journey has been to unlearn the behaviors and ideas that were inhibiting my ability to effectively interact and connect with others.

Going back to past traumas the idea of double-binding also comes to mind from dialogic practice. I had been through incredibly intense experiences in middle school, where I was bullied to the point of nearly committing suicide, and college, where I pledged a fraternity that was perpetually out to hurt me and abuse me and which led to me having psychosis. Being in these situations, I felt I couldn't stand up for myself, and I was given the implicit message that if I did defend myself the situations I was in would worsen substantially. There were two options, neither of which was working, and I had no one to talk with to figure it out. In middle school, I had to go to school so I had no way out and in college for a while I felt I had no place to go. Being in these situations really shut down communication within my mind and broke me down as a person. These were major life events that shadowed the way I viewed myself for many years. Along with being in these situations I also developed the conceptualization practice of giving myself two losing options, and then having no one to talk to about them. This practice was incredibly damaging and I only unlearned it recently. Giving myself productive options that moved past the problem in the way helped me to become a much more fluid thinker and also really improved internal communication. There were also other fears from these situations that arose that came to be unspeakable dilemmas for me. As the years have gone by I've wondered why journaling, which is my primary method of therapy, has worked so well in improving my life, the way I function internally and externally, and my emotional health as well. I've figured out that journaling has been a way of improving communication within my mind.

Within my journaling I've established a number of ways in which I look for wisdom around situations and work towards alleviating the problem in the way. Usually the problem in the way tends to be something that physically causes my forehead to tense up and makes it difficult to speak at times. It can also be the issue that is most present in my mind. There were times I wanted to jump ahead to other issues but I've found when I follow the thought in the way, it usually leads me to the core of a problem that is really deep and needs to be uprooted. Sometimes when I expect to learn about

one problem I learn about something completely different but also something that is incredibly important for
me to learn. I've used a number of techniques that have
worked really well, but the underlying premise is that
they've all helped improve the way I communicate internally and externally. Probably the most noteworthy
of techniques is learning how to forgive others in any
situation where they're not doing right and to still treat
them well. This was the major alleviator I had for lifting
the burden of middle school and the fraternity.

Another important part has just been educating
myself on how social dynamics work and how I can op-
erate well within them. When I initially started journaling I tried removing all the parameters from life, thinking this would open up my mind and give me the freedom I needed. However, I figured out that I needed parameters, but also needed to know when I could break
those rules. Establishing rules within socialization was
incredibly important for improving my mental health,
figuring out what's acceptable and then also giving an
allowance to break rules when need be. I've found good
socialization and communication rules help guide language but they also don't inhibit my ability to break a
rule when I need to. I felt as I developed increasingly
more parameters around what to say and do in social

situations it became a lot easier to know when I could break rules or when I wanted to adhere to them. Knowing the rules of socialization and social dynamics really improved my ability to function socially. The most important part of knowing a good rule is also having an allowance to break it. Good rules for me have enhanced socialization as opposed to creating constraints and limitations that aren't healthy. So a part of this is knowing what is a healthy parameter as opposed to a limiting constraint.

In terms of communication another important part of therapy has been having a good therapist who has been non-judgmental. Judgment and fear shuts down communication so being with someone who was accepting of everything I had gone through really helped improve my mental health. Three primary things I've worked on breaking down in innumerable ways are judgment, hatred, and fear. From my episodes I had many judgments towards people I was interacting with that needed to be broken down to improve communication within my mind. I had many self-judgments as well, as judgment was a primary method that was utilized for a multitude of people who verbally and emotionally bullied me over the years. Intertwined with these judgments were fears. Fears from really intense experiences

126

I had been through, such as nearly being homeless, nearly starving to death, experiencing episodes of psychosis. Being in these intense experiences developed a lot of fears, some of which seemed reasonable, but in the end most of which I was able to refute. Refuting these judgments and fears helped open up communication within my mind. When I was able to prove false a fear I had from an episode it really helped to lift parts of the psychosis. Psychosis for me has been a number of intertwined thought webs which have shut down communication within my mind, primarily composed of fear, hatred, and judgment, so in dialogic terms I see "making movement" as finding ways to lift these fears, judgments, and other impediments to re-establish healthy communication within the mind. At this point I'm still taking medication, but I feel most of my psychosis is gone. Within social situations it feels incredibly easy to know what to say or do whereas for the majority of my life it was incredibly difficult. Socialization never came easy for me so another part of working through psychosis is skill building. I had to build cognitive and emotional skills to help improve internal communication but also to improve interpersonal skills to lift the isolation I had been facing.

The Little Things: A Double Edged Sword
Good Men Project, December 2019

For me, the little things have been a big part of getting healthier from schizoaffective disorder. There were a number of little things that I was doing right but also many that I needed to improve upon. The little things were a double edged sword for me until I learned how to wield them the right way.

As I originally started my journey with recovery from mental illness the little things were incredibly important to me. I was very attentive to doing anything and everything the right way as I thought it was preventing episodes from happening again. A part of me was afraid of making even the slightest of mistakes, so my hyper-vigilance on the little things could be seen as a maladaptive coping mechanism. I felt if I started messing up on the little things it would lead to bigger mistakes. This terrified me because at the time I still had residual thoughts of saving the world and a part of making this happen was doing all the little things the right way. I thought by doing all the little things correctly my thoughts would be disseminated to everyone else thus helping other people to know how to do all the little things.

As I progressed I did realize doing the little things was an important part of getting healthier and I also was able to refute the belief that my thoughts were being disseminated to the rest of the world. Doing the little things right meant helping out at home, doing a good job with anything I was doing, and especially at work with getting the details right. However, after years of doing so I began to learn that my hyper-vigilance with little details had been a problem for many years. The problem was that doing the little things helped give me mental clarity but I also had way too much anxiety over the little things not being done the right way. It was a painful dichotomy that I needed to navigate.

The positives from doing the little things were having a sharper mind, developing positive thinking patterns, and it also clarified my mind a great deal. When I've done the little things correctly it's given me a clear conscience which is an incredibly powerful thing. I realized my memory was sharper, my linguistic ability improved, and my problem solving skills and executive functioning were much more advanced. One of the things I held most firmly to was the clarity of thought I had.

My episodes of schizoaffective disorder made having an unclear mind a very scary thing so anything I could do to clarify my stream of consciousness was very important to me. I had a delusion that not doing the little things the right way would muddle my stream of consciousness and cause me to repeat traumas like going through middle school and pledging the fraternity. Refuting this belief that making mistakes on the little things was okay was incredibly helpful. It was liberating to realize that small mistakes only have small repercussions and they're easily fixed. For me, a matter of knowing when I could make a mistake was thinking in advance of what the consequences of an action might be. Knowing the consequences of actions made me realize that not everything I was doing was going to have any sort of effect on others whatsoever. Dropping a fork on the ground was harmless, leaving the water running too long was not the end of the world, leaving a window cracked when it should be shut was a safe thing to make a mistake on.

One important distinction I had to make was when a little thing was in fact a big deal. Sometimes a seemingly small task has small repercussions but sometimes small tasks can have major repercussions. Small tasks such as leaving the water turned on outside during the winter can create major problems like hundreds of dollars in plumbing damage. Thinking in terms of consequences has been a helpful way to navigate and realize when I'm dealing with a big little thing or when a little thing only has small repercussions.

The other concern I had was if I became too lax with the little things it would lead to bigger problems. I had to realize to some extent this can be true and it's important to pay attention to detail. However, I was putting way too much pressure on myself and it was the pressure of making mistakes on little things that was unhealthy. The pressure I had was that I had to do every little thing right in order to be a writer, have a happy life, and get rid of schizoaffective disorder. The irony of the situation was that the pressure I was putting on myself to do well at these tasks was actually preventing me from completing these tasks as effectively as I could. I learned my hyper-vigilance around the little things was driving people away from me because it caused me to become neurotic when I had fear of a little thing going wrong that didn't make any difference. I also didn't give anyone else any room to make mistakes which made it incredibly difficult for others to be around me. Being difficult to be around led to isolation and isolation amplified my symptoms of schizoaffective.

A part of wisdom is also knowing where to focus our efforts and what things are important to talk about. There were many times I pointed out little mistakes to people that didn't make a difference at all. I thought I was helping but in reality I was turning molehills into mountains. Pointing out innocuous mistakes to people only made them angry and ruined interpersonal relationships for me. I realized an important part of wisdom is what you don't say and it's also about letting the little things go when you can.

Finding a middle ground between allowing mistakes but still getting the little things right was really important for me. This middle ground came through making realizations that little mistakes were not going to lead to bigger issues as long as I generally got the little things correct. I also had to realize that the consequences of the actions I originally assigned to making mistakes on little things was inaccurate. I had a form of magical thinking where I thought little mistakes would have more major repercussions when in reality they don't at all. My thoughts were not being disseminated around the world and having more room for error was a major necessity for me to make more friends, become a better writer, and have a different life perspective. Changing my perspective on mistakes was major. I originally was terrified of making them and now I either look at them as laughable or lessons to learn from. Having a growth mentality as opposed to a fixed mentality helped me to realize mistakes can be a good thing because they can help me grow as a person. The other part about mistakes I realized is that they're unavoidable, and it's a mistake in and of itself to live a life solely for the purpose of not making mistakes. Sometimes mistakes can be the essence of life and can truly make life interesting.

Assumptions and Associations

One of the most important lessons I have learned as a peer specialist and in my recovery is to know the difference between what my assumptions are and also what is truth. After having lived with schizoaffective disorder for twelve years I assumed that my narrative was just like everyone else's and that this was going to make peer-to-peer work easy. I soon learned imposing my narrative on others was frustrating for them because everyone's life story is completely different. As a peer I was taught by my manager that I had to ask more open ended questions and to use my assumptions to lead me to asking open-ended questions. This was very helpful and also got me thinking more about the role of assumptions in thinking.

When I initially tried to figure out how to use my assumptions I tried to get rid of them altogether. Trying this made me momentarily brain dead so I figured out that assumptions are essential to thinking. I realized that projecting myself into the future in terms of living in the present had everything to do with making and fulfilling assumptions. Assumptions are a critical part of thinking because I use them to figure out and move forward in every aspect of my life. In psychology it was difficult to not project my assumptions on others at first but once I realized I could use them to ask open-ended questions I started making progress with people I was working with. I also began making more progress in my own therapy.

I have a journaling process where I remember past thoughts that are problematic and make efforts to turn them into zeros or non-factors in my thinking. In eight years I have had the same amount of medication and my life has completely changed due to this process. My functionality has improved immensely and for a while I had been wondering why this was possible. From a biological standpoint, part of the process is debunking negative thoughts helps my brains communication to improve and this improved neurotransmission helps to improve my functionality. However, I still wondered why I could write something in a journal and it could have an immediate physiological effect and improvement in my mental and emotional health. There are reasons this process works.

In our minds we have two types of basic memories that relate to psychology and improving mental health. One type is all of our experiences which are all stored in our minds from the time we were born and the other type are associations, which are thoughts associated to our memories. Growing up and in college I had a lot of trauma and in therapy I came to the blunt realization that I can't change what had happened to me; that will be forever stored in my mind. However, the process of changing my mental health and improving my functionality came in the form of changing the thoughts I had associated to those traumas. For years I fumbled around with thoughts figuring out what to write and what would help improve my mental health with success but also with failures. I recently realized the thoughts that were easiest to change were the assumptions I had been making due to the traumas I had been through. For example, in middle school I had been picked on to the point of nearly committing suicide. In later years I did a lot of work on changing assumptions I had made based upon my past experiences which were thoughts like getting picked on could lead to suicide. These were subconscious assumptions but had been learned through the experience of trauma. After changing thoughts like these with journaling my mental health and social ability began improving. When I struggled to socialize the false and negative assumptions I had made from middle school trauma were crippling me with social anxiety because every time I was in a social situation I had assumptions deep within my psyche that bad things would happen and this caused a crippling amount of fear. After having this fear I would seize up and struggle to speak. When I was able to change my assumptions this changed my expectations for the social situation and improved the outcomes of the social situations. Removing the fear by removing the assumptions made all the difference in my mental health and I'm now able to socialize effectively.

The other important part about realizing the difference between an assumption and what is actually true had to with the way I was perceiving information. At first if I didn't know the answer to something I would make something up based upon assumptions and feel that I knew the answer. This is a basic process which I've seen a lot of people do but I've learned smarter ways of problem solving and ingesting information. After doing more work with understanding that I myself could not make assumptions when I did not know the answers to questions this helped me to realize how little I truly knew. I had to make certain I wasn't pretending to know the answers to questions when I really didn't have a clue, not make up answers for the sake of sounding smart, and also using facts to ask more questions to get the truest answers. This process helped me to obtain much more accurate information when I was working on my own mental health but also when I was working with others as a peer specialist. I would make assumptions and use those assumptions to ask open-ended questions and after asking the question I would get a reply with an answer that was completely different than the one I expected. The more this happened the more I realized how difficult it was to accurately assume the truth about a myriad of things. Learning a better process of obtaining information helped me to get more accurate information when problem solving and trying to fill in the blanks to peoples' stories.

This improved process of gathering information helped give me a more accurate depiction of the way people think. In the past I would make negative assumptions about people when things didn't work out for them. Once I stopped making assumptions and acting like I understood what everyone was thinking and approached things with an open-mind and asked questions I started reaching better conclusions. In past social situations when something didn't go as planned I made negative assumptions that other people didn't like me or thought poorly of me. In more recent times I've asked questions when plans fell through and didn't make assumptions about people's personalities. When I realized how little I knew and got rid of my assumptions I learned that people cared for me but sometimes things don't always go as planned.

Life with Mental Health Struggles

Forgiving the Psychiatric System
Good Men Project April 2020

In a writing group I've been a part of for over eight years, I was reading an article I'd written about how terrible psychiatric care has been over the centuries. I talked about my own personal experience with things I hear and see within the system and how emotional it is to think about how the conditions are still terrible and not nearly where they need to be. Everyone in the group has known for years that I have had a diagnosis of schizophrenia. In the essay I presented, I spoke about how perplexing and inhumane lobotomies were. I received a response I wasn't expecting. A person who had been in the writing group for over five years —a person whom I liked and trusted — mentioned that she used to take part in lobotomy procedures.

A storm of emotions rose up within me. I felt a rush of anger, hatred, and fear. I felt like a bottle of chemicals that had been shaken furiously. The conditions and the system I had been fighting for years and everything it represented were all sitting at the same table with me and had been doing so for five years without me even knowing it.

The comment was quickly mentioned and because of the rush of emotions that fogged my mind and heart, it was difficult to get a sense of the reasons for it. I held back my emotions as I sat and listened to everyone critiquing the piece. Staring at the bookshelves, I could barely process anything happening in the room and surges of white noise cluttered my stream of consciousness. My heart was on fire and I did everything I could to remain respectful. My responses were short and curt as I couldn't muster the equanimity to comprise more fluid, logical, and articulate answers. Afterwards, everyone was going out together. I almost didn't go. I didn't want to be anywhere within the same zip code as the individual who had mentioned she had practiced lobotomies. I felt a surge of disgust and a longing to be as far away from her as possible. After she had mentioned her past to me, I saw her in a completely different way. I said very few words during a two hours stretch to a person whom I had been very friendly with for five years. It wasn't even necessarily out of principle or choice, I just was not mentally and emotionally able to hold a conversation with her. I left that night, wondering if I'd ever even return to spend time with that group.

The next week I saw my psychiatrist and mentioned the incident to him. I vented about how infuriating the entire situation was and I received a response I didn't expect. "What would it take to forgive her?" I laughed a little bit as I knew there was some wisdom in this. My doctor has a way of contradicting me when I need it the most. I humorously thought of the movie BraveHeart where the Scottish yell "You Bastard" as I had been deprived of my anger and had it replaced with some laughter.

For a little over two weeks I was furious and I felt the burden of hatred and anger coursing through me intermittently throughout my days. It took many conversations with coworkers at my hospital, two therapy appointments, and a lot of journaling to gain enough wisdom around the situation to see things more clearly. I think I first had to experience the negative emotions to move towards the positive ones. After experiencing them for long enough I realized how much of a burden they were. My negative emotions and all the fury of the world that accompanied it, finally dissipated after I began thinking about what forgiveness would look like. The human condition only allows us to live in the present while projecting ourselves into the future.

This simply means that none of us are capable of changing the past. No matter how much anger and hatred I had, it wasn't going to change anything. Lobotomies aren't happening anymore, the person who had participated in them had walked away free along with everyone else in the past several centuries who did so as well. Thinking about the situation, a part of me wanted justice. However, what would justice look like and how would that even be brought about? Having known this person, I know she definitely had some emotional struggles throughout her life. Was the weight of having to live with her crimes enough to prevent them from ever happening again? Apparently something had changed over the past forty years as lobotomies are no longer practiced. The procedure was listed as a medical procedure even though in my mind it seems more like a crime against humanity. Ideally, there would be some commemoration and justice sought for the thousands of lives ruined by this procedure and its' crudeness.

I realized there was something far more important that needed to happen. Forgiveness gave me the ability to move forward and to let go of most of my anger and hatred I felt. In terms of the mental health civil rights movement, I think it's important for us to remember all of this. Remember it, so it doesn't happen again. Remember it, so we can guide ourselves to a better future. However, even more importantly, I don't see human suffering as having boundaries and some people deserving freedom from it more so than others. If the goal of the movement is to end suffering, forgiveness needs to be a part of it. I don't want her to suffer for things she can't change, including the lobotomies. I don't want her to carry that emotional pain with her anymore. Throughout the entire five years I've known her, she's always taken good care of me and she's had my best interest in mind, and we've really enjoyed each others' company. If one person is suffering, we're all suffering and I'd like her to know I do forgive her for having been a part of lobotomies and I hope she's able to forgive herself.

Looking back, there is another side to the story. As crude as the history of psychiatry is, there's been a problem with the system, and not entirely with the people. The systems put in place, created conditions where lobotomies happened and the other hellacious elements were also thrown into the mix. Without forgiving people for the things they did in a system that made them believe they were doing the right things and helping people, we're only creating opposition. Without allowing people to forgive themselves, they're not fully able to make amends with their pasts and become a part of the solution. Together we're united, separated we fail. A society's ability to forgive is the fabric that keeps it together. Keeping us all together and progressing towards improving the system is going to be the only thing that continues to catalyze change.

Philosophy and Life Events; Keys to Alleviating Depression

Good Men Project, January 2020

Bipolar disorder has been a major part of my mental health journey and one of the more difficult components to this has been depression. Until recently I didn't know the extent of the negativity I was experiencing emotionally. I've started to climb out of the negative side of bipolarity in a healthy way. Some of this has had to do with eliminating life stressors, while another facet of it has been developing wiser ways of viewing the world.

A major component to my negative thoughts and emotions was circumstantial. For a while I was struggling to maintain regular social contacts, get along with my family, and I was barely getting by financially. These were major life stressors that were major detriments to my mental health. I worked hard on improving my social skills but I still struggled interpersonally. The constant stress of worrying about every small expense as being an important decision caused me depression, anger, and this fueled some of my other symptoms as well including psychosis. When I was in these negative states it was difficult to have positive social interactions because I unintentionally transferred all my life stress to my social and familial conversations. This made spending time with me a burden to others mentally and emotionally because of all my negativity. At the time I couldn't see that I needed to change, however, I don't blame people for limiting their social contact with me during these times. I can see how it can be difficult to interact with me when I was in my most negative states. As I worked on my social skills I began getting along better with family and friends but finances were still a major life stressor. "Anyone who has ever struggled with poverty knows how extremely expensive it is to be poor" (James Baldwin). Not having good financial standing caused me to want to work as hard as I could on my mental health around the clock. Every day I took a number of measures to make my bills cheaper, to find ways of saving, and to cut my spending in as many ways as I possibly could.

Part of my issue has been that reading causes psychosis for me so every day after working eight to nine hours with two hours of commuting I got home and continued to work to solve this problem and to work on alleviating my psychosis. It's something I've made great progress on but it still affects me. Being a peer specialist, I could get by with the amount of reading I had at work while still having some symptoms, but my thoughts have been if I was able to read it alleviates the burden of being limited to peer work if I ever needed to switch careers to make a better salary. One day, I crossed an incredible stroke of like which was life altering. It was determined at work that peer salaries were well under where they should be and we all were increased by four dollars per hour. It felt miraculous as my day to day financial worries were alleviated. At my previous salary I was right around break even financially with all my expenses but now I had disposable income. Having the disposable income and being financially stable alleviated a great deal of stress. With my financial worries liquidated, I could breathe and my negative emotions, anger, and irritability all decreased. I now had more disposable income to do more fun things, eat healthier food, pick up the check at a restaurant, go out to eat if I needed to, get gas at a more expensive station if it was more convenient, and not be stressed about every single expenditure as a major financial decision. Having money does alleviate stress and it's not the entirety of being happy but having enough of it certainly does help. Money does create happiness to an extent. However, there was still a great deal of negativity remaining that needed to be resolved.

In supervision, I was told to not attribute malice to a mistake when it could just be stupidity. This was put bluntly but opened up a number of avenues for improvement. I built off this concept and also figured to not attribute bad intentions where there are good, ill will where there is good will, a reasonable explanation as opposed to an unreasonable one, and also to look for greater reasons for people's mistakes other than simplistic explanations of incompetence. This paradigm shift clarified life for me immensely and I started drawing much better conclusions when thinking about everything in my life. My conclusions were healthier and much closer to the truth. In the past, if someone cut me off in traffic I'd get angry and yell that they were stupid. Now I make the conjecture that maybe they just didn't see me and it's not a problem which to me is a more reasonable answer. Even if they did cut me off maybe they were just in a hurry and there was no ill will intended. Thoughts like these have made it easier to forgive people but also to understand there's more to situations than simple answers. I was looking for simple answers, in terms of identifying and vilifying a particular individual who seemed to be wrong as bad, myself as good, thus giving me someone to direct my anger towards and fueling negative emotions. However, when I was able to see most people have good intentions and mean well, even if the consequences of their actions don't pan out that way, but also that not everything is a question of morality, this helped me see the causality of people's mistakes in a much clearer light.

There were so many times I attributed a person's morality as the reasons to their shortcomings, especially my own, but when I realized there are far more factors and components to a problem than I could even compute it took the onus off myself and others. The problems were still my responsibility to solve but it didn't necessarily matter where the fault fell. Fault could be redistributed solely from myself and reallocated to a number of sources for any problem. This alleviated depression immensely because in the past if I messed up I was really hard on myself but at this point I see that maybe there was more happening than I could process at the time of a mistake. Knowing this also helped me to realize that in life, we sometimes have to make the mistake that's in the way, and this has also helped me emotionally. I realize in life, based upon what I've learned up to a certain point I'm bound to make mistakes that are unavoidable. Using these as learning opportunities and looking at mistakes as learning opportunities also took the pressure off myself in these situations. With this major shift in my thinking, my conversations were becoming healthier and easier to conduct. People were beginning to want to spend more time with me and to enjoy being around me. In the past when I was lamenting about how I thought everyone in the world was bad people didn't want to be around me. My conversations have become more positive and this has made it easier for people to spend time with me. Alleviating my isolation has made me happier and I haven't felt depressed for a while now.

The depression had more to do with the way I was conceptualizing life, mistakes, and situations in life than it did with who I was as a person. However, changing the way I conceptualized life helped me grow in ways I couldn't even imagine. I think another component to keep in mind was that the problem also had to do with my financial situation and life circumstances. It's important to realize how life circumstances can be a major cause of emotional conditions as well as having been through difficult life experiences and needing to change philosophically.

The Will To Truth: Existentialism and Psychosis

Good Men Project, November 2019

Over the years it took me time to not view myself from a stigmatic vantage point. I had learned many false notions from popular culture, conversations throughout my life, and from medical staff as well. Getting rid of stigma I had towards myself has been a big step in improving my mental health.

When I made my first in-patient stay at a local hospital I was absolutely terrified of the doctor. He was stern and cold and in my mind he represented doctors who I had seen in movies and TV. He was not the least bit personable and I wasn't able to make a connection to him. His decision to intentionally disconnect from me fed into my belief that I was less human at that moment. It fed into the feeling of being an other and inferior and being a unit that needed treatment as opposed to a person who needed to get his life back. From the start of care there was a seed planted in my mind that he was the doctor, I was the patient, and that I was a problem that needed to be solved. I began viewing myself as a problem that needed to be solved which was a difficult way to go through the world.

Hearing the diagnosis that I had schizophrenia was even more terrifying. I pushed it away at first because of all the stigma surrounding the word. In later years I figured out that schizophrenia was a word to encompass the symptoms I had already experienced and nothing additional was going to happen. Realizing this was a major relief but it took about two years. These symptoms came in the form of having disorganized thinking, some obsessive compulsive behaviors, occasionally seeing and hearing things, sleeplessness, extreme highs and lows emotionally, and experiencing a multitude of anxiety that made me unable to speak, think, and process language at times. For me schizoaffective disorder has been nothing more than these things. Originally hearing the word schizophrenia associated with my identity worried me that I would become like people I had seen in the movies and on television. Over time I figured out that I wasn't anything like those people and no one with psychosis really is.

Not viewing myself as a problem to be solved took even more years of work to unravel. I had read Nietzsche and deep within my mind was the "will to power" also known as the "will to truth". I believed my ability to find the truth was going to lead me out of the depths of my schizophrenia symptoms which was partially true. However, over the years I developed a rigid belief system that was solely focused on finding the deepest truth within any and every situation which was damaging. This became a major barrier in connecting to others and being able to have a good social life. I had some individual friends but I was in a lot of pain.

I originally thought I was in a lot of pain because of the traumatic experiences that caused the illness but I learned for myself that the experiential side of the illness is a series of judgments and fears interconnected with pain from traumatic experiences. To break down these thought webs I couldn't get rid of my "will to truth" necessarily but I had to learn some better social skills and priorities surrounding my will to truth and the purpose for it as well. When working on getting healthier, I still had to give myself absolute truths but I had to learn the time and place to do so in conversations with others. I had to learn to put everyone else's health and well-being as well as my own before my desire to know the truth and my desire for others to know the truth. There were many instances I should have let things go and I should have allowed people to say and do the wrong things however I was correcting everything everyone was saying. I also learned that there are many truths about a situation that can be shared and you don't have to give someone an absolute truth to get through a conversation where you are in disagreement. I thought I only had to ingest good information to get to the absolute deepest truths so that I could recover from schizoaffective disorder. I also thought that other people needed the truth all the time so that they could improve as well.

The irony of the situation was that in some instances I needed the truth, but my "will to truth" was a source of pain and suffering. It kept me distant from everyone in my life. Once I began figuring out that I'm a human being first who is allowed to and should enjoy life and that solving problems comes afterwards I began connecting to others much better. Much of my illness was structured around my desires to write, help others, and to keep improving. I had to learn people's feelings, emotions, and wellbeing always come before the truth and that these things are the purpose for the truth. This set me free from my self-destructing desire to constantly find truth and to tell people truths that they didn't need to hear. The truth is an instrument to help us become healthier, not to constrain us and trap us within obsessive rituals. The more I deconstructed the thought webs of striving towards intellectual excellence the healthier I became and as I became healthier my writing improved in ways it otherwise wouldn't have been able to.

This created a paradigm shift in seeing myself in a more human way as opposed to a problem that needed to be solved. I decided my life has to come before my writing and my work. Before this I had been living a lifestyle of efficiency, minimalism, perfectionism, and conditioning myself with behavioral and cognitive practices just for the sake of improving my writing. Unlearning this was incredibly helpful to feeling better and getting healthier and when I learned that everyone's health and wellness come first, including my own, it alleviated the mental restraints I had self-imposed upon myself. I had to unlearn what I thought was self-help to liberate my mind.

Self-Perceptions: Motivation and Detriments to Mental Health Recovery

Schizoaffective Disorder has been an illness that has given me a variety of self-perceptions. There were self-perceptions that were positive, helpful, detrimental, negative, symptom-provoking, and just a wide range of ways I viewed myself. Utilizing self-perceptions has been a helpful tool in recovering and reaching a point of having a full life.

After my second episode I didn't have any friends, a job, I had thought blocking, poor executive functioning, and I struggled with many symptoms. This slew of problems created poor self-esteem which fueled more symptoms. Stress has always been the lynchpin for symptoms for me therefore the more I self-deprecated, the more my stress increased thus amplifying my symptoms. Initially I was poorly equipped to handle the illness. However, I was working for an insurance company making a decent paycheck. I had suicidal thoughts daily so I decided to sponsor a child. I thought if I can't work and live for myself I'll have to at least do so for someone else. This helped improve my emotional health enough to make me feel worth while and to alleviate suicidal thoughts. I felt if I was helping someone else then I was deserving of self-help and I felt motivated to work hard in therapy.

Eventually I was unable to sponsor the child and needed new motivation. This time I turned to writing. I felt if I was doing what I could to help other people with my writing, they would benefit, but I would also be more deserving of the self-help I needed. I realized as I got healthier I was able to divulge my findings to others and help more people thus the fire was fueled. Writing became a catalyst for self-help even when my self-esteem was still lacking. As long as I was writing I had a reason to keep working on and improving myself. During this time I still had many suicidal thoughts and writing was keeping me alive. I had to keep writing to take care of myself and keep taking care of myself to write. It was a vicious cycle that fueled me through some really difficult traumas, however, it worked in some ways. A good writing friend always mentioned to me, "There is no greater motivation than duty." Having a responsibility to others, people who read my writing, made me feel that I was a part of something and gave me a feeling of connection. That feeling of connection came from a shared pain that I knew others were experiencing. I didn't want anyone to have to go through what I went through.

Every time I wrote I vowed to put forth my best effort. I wasn't going to lay down and allow mental illness to plague myself or as many people as I could help escape from it. This created meaning and purpose in my life. I felt there were people who needed me even when I felt I wasn't needed and this helped me persist.

With enough self-esteem to at least keep me going I still had other self-perceptions that worked for and against me. Being someone who was going to thrive as opposed to being a victim was important. Early on in recovery I prayed for help and hoped that somehow things would magically change. After months of this I came to a grave realization that I was the only one who was going to get myself out of this pit. I read Victor Frankl's "Man's Search for Meaning" as recommended by my doctor and his book changed my life. I had help but I decided I just wasn't going to let the illness control my life. That one day, I'd live a life worth while and I didn't care what it took to get there. I dictated that I would thrive and live just as well as anyone and that began my work on my mental health. I decided to declare war against my mental illness. I was going to attack it from all angles until I fully expunged the experiential side or at least had a life I felt was worth while.

I created a self-perception that my life would be just as good as anyone's who did not have any trauma and/or schizoaffective disorder. This caused me to hold myself to high standards in all areas in my life. It was a double-edged quality that worked for and against me. There were times I still had too much trauma affecting me and I wasn't able to function and socialize the same way everyone around me was. It was painful because I wasn't able to live up to the standards I was holding myself to; those being that I am no different than anyone else and I can be the same as them. On the other hand it motivated me to work hard in my journaling at home and in therapy to get to a point where I could be on par with anyone in terms of mental and emotional health and have the same quality of life if not better.

I did this for years and it was painful to keep falling short of the expectations of being as healthy as others. I fell short time and time again but I did my best to fall forward every time. Falling towards my goals I eventually realized I had to ease up on myself. I had the belief that I had to be hard on my-self to create desire and to fuel my recovery. I soon realized it was much healthier to be kind and have self-compassion and that my mental health improved at much faster rates too. My progress when I learned from mistakes as opposed to self-deprecating compounded quickly. I could be just as motivated to excel when I was self-forgiving than if I was self-deprecating. I learned I had to pick myself up with ease when I fell short of my expectations but to still work towards getting better. Mistakes didn't have to be opportunities for abuse, I just needed to learn from them and self-deprecation did not have to be incorporated with learning.

Lastly, after making enough progress to get to a point where I felt my life was better and that I would go on to be okay, I still felt insatiable. The pain was still there. I think our society has ways of projecting insatiability on us for a number of reasons but it was something I had to unlearn. The insatiability was a self-perception I had been taught from a young age. "Never be satisfied", "always want more", "keep improving". Realizing that gratitude doesn't create complacency was incredibly helpful. When I dispelled the notion that satisfaction, gratitude and a desire to improve could co-exist I felt immensely relieved. For years I hadn't been able to celebrate my life successes and mental health improvement because I was afraid. I was afraid that having gratitude would create complacency and complacency would lead me to having my health deteriorate thus bringing me back to where I started. Learning that gratitude and a will to improve are good life partners helped me to feel good about the progress I had made while still working towards projecting myself out of a cave that perpetually becomes brighter. (Plato)

Losing and Regaining Faith
Good Men Project, April 2018

While I was growing up I had an unwavering belief in divinity and faith. When everything was going well it was easy for me to hold fast to the religious principles I was brought up with. I believed in God, heaven, the afterlife, and pretty much most of what I was taught in religious school. However, this all changed during my episodes.

During my first episode of schizoaffective disorder I believed that I was an agent of divinity that would have to do everything correctly to save the world. I laugh today because the world still hasn't quite "been saved" but it's also a pretty good place in a lot of regards. This notion that I was a messiah may have actually kept me alive during an episode where I nearly starved to death and slept on the tile floor of a very cold apartment in the middle of a New England winter while experiencing a full on psychotic episode. My belief that I had to save the world motivated me to persist against bleak odds and complete my college course work as an English major for that semester during this episode.

However, I had one more episode and after this episode I began making a journey away from spirituality. One of my main problems was that I wanted to believe in divinity and the great beyond but I had a lot of questions regarding what I had been through. Growing up, I basically believed that if I had done everything the right way, which I thought I did, then I would be taken care of by the watchful presence of the divine. However, after two episodes of schizoaffective disorder I challenged this belief and started thinking that no one was watching over me because of all the pain and adversity I was forced to go through by no fault of my own. I had a lot more to learn about life.

For several years I wasn't even willing to say a prayer. I thought it was more important for me to find ways to make my life change instead of praying for hope. I didn't understand the power of prayer and/or the reason for it. My notion was that when I previously prayed I was just hoping for everything to change without implementing any actions which of course didn't work. I didn't realize that sometimes prayer is just a way of being heard. I came to learn that prayer is a good way to express gratitude and to have an ongoing conversation with someone that possibly goes beyond the earth. I wasn't certain whether there was a great beyond or any Gods for a while but I learned that praying made me feel good about life so I began doing it more. I liked to pray in thanks for things I was grateful for and also send my regards to relatives who had previously passed on from this life. It felt good in my heart and my mind so I continued to do it. It seemed to hold intrinsic value.

One main issue I had was with my delusion of becoming a messiah. Since trying to become a messiah lead to so many problems during my episodes I had a natural disinclination towards believing in divinity or anything religious. I understood afterwards that I wasn't a messiah but I still had to extract that delusion from my belief system. For me delusions tend to stick around until they're addressed regardless of how irrational they were. I thought it was problematic to have belief in the divine because of the delusion of thinking I was a messiah that had influenced so many actions in my episodes that were unhealthy and dangerous. When I addressed the issue that I'm not a messiah nor do I need to be one this fear of religion began to fade away. I worked on realizing that I just have to take care of the things within my sphere of influence and that it's up to everyone to do this in their own life. It's not up to me to do it for them or to save the masses with super human powers. When I learned to just take care of what I could and not worry about things and people that were not within my sphere of influence my delusions of wanting to be a messiah were quelled.

There were times when I questioned whether there even could be life after earth. In some ways I looked at all the factors that went into the creation of the earth and juxtaposed two different beliefs. On one hand it seems as though everything was designed and created for reasons to balance and check each other. The earth seemed like a place that was created by great mathematician(s) and or creator(s) because of all the varying factors that had to come together perfectly for life on earth to exist. On the other hand it could have all just been accidental and a lot of this could have to do with the way the human mind works, always searching for connections between things that may or very well may not be connected. The consensus I came to was that praying and having faith made me feel too good to not have any belief in it. It helped me to pray and have faith for my emotional health and overall well-being.

After making this decision that there may very well have been some sort of creator(s) who put the earth together I wondered why I went through so much adversity if I had been doing everything the right way. I had always been told if I do the right thing everything will work out. If I'm a good person then life will be good. One thing I learned that I was not a perfect person and that no one is and I wasn't actually doing everything correctly. I realized that I do have free will and in my mind no one would necessarily create me without giving me free will. I guess I had to challenge the belief that divinity had a plan for my life. This works differently for different people but for me it helped me to believe I was now in control of my own life. I could project a course I would want to embark on and make plans and implement agency to create positive change in my life. Once I became more adept at doing this I came to the notion that if a grande creator was to put me into life that the whole purpose of me having life was a gift. It was something that was meant for me to guide and control and figure out, and not necessarily just sit on a roller coaster ride and enjoy the view. This helped me to let go of the notion that the grande creator(s) who I had so strongly believed in as a child had not

168

abandoned me at all. This was because I now felt that they were not in control of my life and only I was. I think a part of this was also being more mentally awake as an adult as opposed to my episodes where I wasn't very mentally awake at all. Believing that divinity had no control over my life whatsoever really helped me to let go of the pain I had felt of being abandoned in my darkest hours.

Overall, I realized that the earth isn't perfect and there's no such thing as a perfect person being created. In my mind I learned that I am flawed and maybe our creator(s) are also flawed. The thing I came to believe which helped me to regain my faith in some sort of creator(s) and/or after life was that the earth is a place of free will. Life is a gift either created scientifically or by some sort of divine intelligence however, either way, life is ours to live and the purpose of faith is to help us to influence our lives in a way that is as positive as possible. I learned if there are higher powers then they didn't create us for the sake of controlling our every move. One of the greatest things about life is being in the arena and learning, living, and experiencing and overcoming the trials and tribulations that life brings to the table. I found that faith is a tool to help me through some of this adversity and that my life is in my own hands. I was brought back to faith by realizing I have to use the agency I was created with to implement the good lessons I had learned from the number of religions and schools of thought I have studied.

Disclosing a Diagnosis While Dating

Getting back into the dating world after having schizoaffective disorder for thirteen years has been a new and interesting challenge. I did have a girlfriend about four years ago for six months but since then I've just worked on my mental health. I had a lot of insecurities that I've been learning how to navigate.

For a while I didn't know whether being a peer specialist was something I wanted to mention to anyone I was just meeting for the first time. I liked to tell people I'm a mental health counselor as this was ambiguous and equivocal but avoided questions. I figured if I tell people I'm a peer counselor they may ask where do you work. I work for the psychotic disorders division of a psychiatric hospital so it would basically be disclosing my mental illness. Ideally, I'd be able to say this without being judged. Even at a recent WRAP Training with clinicians in attendance I was three quarters of the way through without disclosing my diagnosis. Everyone was friendly and kind to me and towards the end we did a "speed dating" session where we set up the chairs accordingly and just met everyone in the training and talked to them. As I disclosed I was a peer to a number of people and I worked in the psychotic disorders division the conversations changed almost as soon as I spoke the words. Some people got it and didn't care, others were overly nice or concerned, some were fearful. I received a number of reactions most of which weren't good. Experiences like this have taught me that as much as I would like to be able to live freely and openly I'm still forced to live somewhat of a secret life. I'm comfortable with the diagnosis that categorizes my symptoms and experiences but other people have negative associations to the words schizoaffective, schizophrenia, psychosis, and this causes them to treat me differently.

With dating, I thought if I was up front about the work I do, most women wouldn't be interested. I figured there were so many people messaging them that they would never stop for a peer counselor, part of which doesn't pay well, part of which divulges I've had mental health struggles, part of which I had my own self-consciousness towards. So as I started dating I just said I was a mental health counselor as opposed to saying I was a peer counselor. I had a lot of fear that disclosing my diagnosis would prevent people from seeing me for who I am which has been my experience a number of times in the past.

172

I started dating a really nice girl who also works in mental health. We clicked right away and we were having fun. She knew a lot about psychology so she asked me what my credentials were and I made a pretty bad mistake. I lied to her and told her I had an LMHC because I was worried telling her I'm a peer counselor on the first date would cause her to not want to be with me. My full intentions were for her to just get to know me and then I'd tell her about my diagnosis and my job, which I am very proud of. I wanted her to see me for who I am as opposed to framing me the way others did and treating me awkwardly, inhumanely, and not with equality. So we've dated for three weeks and eventually I found a place in the conversation where I had to just be honest with her. It came well before I was comfortable. A part of me looks back and wonders at what point would I ever have been comfortable disclosing my diagnosis to someone new. Especially after having lied. It's never been an easy thing for me to do and even at work when I tell people my diagnosis they're sometimes awkward and treat me differently.

I told her my diagnosis and I told her my true job title and she reacted a lot differently than I thought. I thought she would be okay with everything, however, the one thing she wasn't okay with me on was the lying.

The diagnosis she didn't seem to care about at all. She was really upset that I lied to her which I fully understood. I tried to explain to her about all the stigma in popular culture and about these conversations I've had that I've mentioned earlier.

She mentioned two of her core values are honesty and integrity which are also my core values. She started reiterating questions she had previously asked me on other dates to check the validity of my answers. The job title was the only thing I had lied about as I don't like lying either. I surprisingly started getting a little frustrated. My integrity was being questioned in a situation where I had to defend myself. I've always had a great deal of integrity but she didn't understand the amount of stigma I've had to deal with and the different ways I've been treated because of it. She couldn't see why I would lie to her about something incredibly personal that I thought would drive her away before she got a chance to know me. My other fear was that she'd get to know me and disclosing the diagnosis would change the way she treated me, which is a question that is still unanswered.

After having this conversation I felt terrible. She told me about the amount of dates she had been on where people had lied to her. I also felt upset that she wasn't able to see the reasons why I told her this. It made me wonder what might be the right thing to do going forward. I know I don't ever want to lie to anyone however, does every person react the same way she would? And would every person still treat me the same way? Do people have a right to know about my mental health up front? Part of me wonders whether she was lying to me saying she still would have been interested in me if I disclosed my diagnosis upfront. She told me she wouldn't have cared and it wouldn't have mattered to her but it's hard to believe there wasn't some self-deceit. I still don't know if it really would or wouldn't have bothered her or if she was just saying that. I felt like I didn't get a fully honest response and instead I got a more socially acceptable one. I think another part of me wonders how many people are open-minded enough to truly be on the right page with my diagnosis or how many people just say they are when asked. Most of my friends have treated me the same but with them I let them get to know me first then I told them the diagnosis. Even after telling some of them about my mental health they still sometimes say awkward things around me about mental health.

It made me realize several things. I had to see my value as a person and realize if someone doesn't like me for who I am maybe they're not someone I want to be with. If someone isn't willing to accept my mental health up front is this the type of person I'd like in my life? I realized my fear of being judged immensely influenced my decision to lie to her. So where do I stand? Am I open to anyone and everyone knowing about my diagnosis and fly through the flak that accompanies it wherever I go? I don't think this is a good way of doing things.

In retrospect I think I could have just kept with being a mental health counselor and not lied about the job title. In a way I am a mental health counselor. After processing the situation more I think it was my own insecurities that got in the way of me telling the truth. As I processed more times in the past where people were awkward towards me I think some of it was because I was socially awkward and didn't have anything to do with the diagnosis. However, there are other times where people just had stigma. On the other hand, it's also difficult to believe that as anyone is scrolling through a match profile and they see peer counselor that judgments don't come to mind immediately and with the multitude of people online the individual keeps scrolling to someone with a different job title, if they even bothered to read the rest of the profile. I think I still have a right to control who does or doesn't know about my mental health, not to mention that divulging you're a peer counselor and having a conversation about work leads to divulging my diagnosis which has stopped conversations in the past.

Another important learning curve for me was honesty in a relationship. Trust is essential and lying to her definitely pushed her away, regardless of the diagnosis. I think it's a tough situation because being a peer specialist forces me to disclose my diagnosis right away. If I was in another profession my mental health wouldn't be a part of the conversation but as a peer my mental health is essential to the work I do everyday. In terms of where I stand I don't know the right answer for talking about my work in dating contexts. I'm definitely all about being honest and knowing the truth will come out but I wonder why I have to put so much thought into figuring out a way someone can see me for who I am despite my diagnosis, without stigma factoring into their decision of whether or not they want to date me.

Reuniting Father & Son; One Match at a Time
Good Men Project, July 2016

Following five years of schizoaffective disorder episodes, I had trouble communicating with my Dad. I had forgotten all the good things he had done for me and I had blamed him for things that weren't his fault. I wanted to posit responsibility for having a mental illness on something, or someone, not knowing exactly what it was. I was disoriented and in an adverse state of mind and I directed this confusion towards him. It wasn't fair, and it was a completely inaccurate assessment, but it was the way things were.

Fortunately, we still had a lot of common interests including the game of golf. Growing up we had always gone golfing together and he had showed me every nuance of the game. It's always been his favorite sport. It's been a way of life and through it he's taught me a great deal about life.

During this rocky period while I was living at home after my episodes, we talked very infrequently. Even while watching sports there was very little conversation and I spent a great deal of time alone.

I struggled to reintegrate into society because I had been in isolation for the past five years and I had a lot of issues re-learning socialization. My Dad made certain to bring me to the golf course with he and his friends every weekend so we could spend quality time together and also so I had people to hang out with. His friends were all his age but they all treated me like a son and they helped to momentarily clear the clouds that weathered my life day in and day out for 4 hours playing eighteen holes.

During the beginning of this process we were playing Portsmouth Country Club, which was our favorite course. It was late day and a bright yellowy orange sun sat back behind number 16 which was a par 3. I struck a pitching wedge about 140 yards, dropping it several feet in front of the hole. Rolling forward inch by inch the ball approached the hole, narrowly missing an ace and proceeding to stop about ten feet above the hole. My dad on the other hand, had seen the shot. He saw the way the ball had traveled and he knew what to hit. His shot sailed high and far and dropped down at nearly the same spot mine did. Rolling forward the ball seemed to have disappeared but we couldn't tell because the sun was blinding.

With high hopes we hopped into the cart and approached the hole. I ran to the cup, looked down, and realized my Dad had just made his first ever hole in one at age 54. I hugged him close and there were tears in both our eyes. It was a powerful moment. I couldn't have been happier that I was there to see his first ever ace and I know he wouldn't have wanted it any other way. This moment showed me how much he cared about me and it also reminded me how much I cared for him.

However, the hole wasn't over. During this 18 hole match between father and son, son having taken many a beatings in the past in golf, there were strokes to be given. At the time I was an eighteen handicap and my Dad was a four so I was stroking on that hole. Not knowing this I stepped up to my ball and took my read on the putt. If I hit the putt correctly, the ball would break several inches and coast down hill hitting the cup right center. Stepping over the ball with the hangover of high emotions from the hole-in-one, I didn't care if it dropped or didn't drop. The day was over in my mind and there was nothing that could make it any better. No pressure, no reason to worry that I might leave this birdie putt halfway, or top the ball, or just completely shank the putt. I stepped up, and struck the putt well, drilling it center cup. I halved the hole on my Dad's first ever hole-in-one. After realizing he didn't win the hole with an ace we laughed harder than ever.

"You halved the hole, you mutt," my father said to me.

I replied telling him that even a hole-in-one isn't good enough to out-do the new and improved Steve Colori. After the hangover of emotions we went to the next tee to finish up with 17 and 18. Unbeknownst to my father, he teed off with the hole-in-one ball. Luckily, we found the ball. This sparked another good laugh and after 18 we turned into the clubhouse for a beer. I also made certain to tell everyone the story of my father's hole-in-one. How his son couldn't be beat, how important it was to be there for such an awesome moment, how I wouldn't have had it any other way.

Sometimes it's not necessarily important to sort through all the tough times, figure out who's to blame, what's to fix, or who should've done better. We never got into who was right, or who was wrong, or what needed to change and what didn't. That would have been an extremely difficult con-versation to have. Instead we just kept golfing, con-tinued making new memories thus washing away several rocky years by moving along a current that eventually lead to a better shore. That current was powered by things like golfing together, going to games, and simply spending time together enjoying common interests. Some messages aren't spoken with words.

I eventually realized my Dad loves me and I wrongfully blamed him for having had schizoaffective disorder. To this day I'm uncertain of the cause of the illness and I don't know if I'll ever figure that out; some of it's biological and some experiential. However, I did figure out that we needed to mend the relationship that had been harried by my illness. We're now closer than ever and we continue to play a lot of golf, watch sports, and remind one another of the hole-in-one that didn't win the hole.

Working While Rehabbing

Schizophrenia Bulletin by Oxford Medical Journals,
July 2015

After experiencing my second episode of
schizoaffective disorder, I had difficulty finding
meaningful and productive activities to pursue. I
spent a great deal of time sitting on the couch
watching TV and despairing over having schizoaffective disorder and the state of life it had created
for me which was a friendless and lonely place
where I had nothing going for me, was lethargic,
and lame from inactivity. I had a college degree but
I wasn't at the point where I felt I could handle a job
with work commensurate to that which I had com-
pleted in college. I realized I can't do this for the
rest of my life and something needs to change.

Over the years I've noticed when I've spent
too much time idling it's caused my self-esteem to
drop, my mind has become duller, my social interactions lack luster, I have felt off emotionally, and
my body has felt lethargic. Over-idling has also
caused me to feel a lack of motiva- tion to pursue
any activities that hold any meaning and has made
my life feel meaningless as a result. I realized this

during my time in the basement and decided I needed any job I could get. I was sitting and thinking too much about everything that had just happened and this was detrimental for a number of reasons. Working helped me to focus outwards and get me outside of my mind because I was interacting and focusing externally instead of being locked in reverie. Simply being forced to interact with others helped me develop socialization skills. It got me moving around again and helped me lose weight. My self-esteem also improved simply from having a paycheck and also from the meaningfulness any respectable occupation tends to provide.

I needed about 6 months after my second episode to get to a point where I could function and socialize effectively enough to work. I still had a great deal of social anxiety and awkward moments but obtaining work helped me get through this. Although I wasn't ready to work in an office or in a more intellectual job, I determined I still needed some sort of work just to feel a little more productive. I still had many issues and I knew it so I wanted to ensure I was n't overwhelmed by a full week of work after having spent the past year or so being unemployed. I looked for a job with 20–30 h per week.

I decided I first need to develop a resume, which I did with the help of my sister who is an HR professional. We listed my college degree and past working experiences and organized it well. I'm always grateful I had her help because I don't think I would have been able to write as good a resume without her assistance. An important part of over-coming mental illness, or just reaching any goals in life, has been using the resources available to me to the best of my ability. My sister was one re-source, and for job searches there are others. For people with disabilities there are clubhouses which can be contacted via inter- net or phone. These are real places where people can go daily to rehabili-tate their working and socialization skills. They have programs where you can learn and perform job tasks which help train you to reenter the work force. There are also rehabilitation services and assistance pro- grams for obtaining a degree or job training to start a career in a trade. As far as sim-pler jobs they usually have connections with local businesses that can directly assist you in obtaining an interview and obtaining entry-level jobs. I didn't use the club house to obtain my first job after college, which was working at K-Mart, but I later found people I had been working with had used the clubhouse to gain employment at my same store.

With a decent resume and basic socialization skills I was able to obtain an interview at K-Mart. An impor- tant part of the interviewing process was informing the company that I wanted to move up within their ranks. Another important facet of the interview process was dressing appropriately. I wore a button down shirt with a tie and a black pant but wearing a suit to that interview might have lost me the job. While applying to higher positions a suit worked well but I think the attire needs to match the title of the job and I was applying for store associate. During the interview I was conscientious and sociable but most importantly I was honest. Human Resources managers are fairly smart and most of them are able to determine if you are telling the truth. I using concrete information from past work experiences to sup- port my answers which helped me obtain the job. For example, they asked if I was physically able to complete the work and I did have some strength which was visible, but I also cited how I had landscaped for 3 years dur- ing college which supported my credential. I'll usually put relevant work experience on the resume if applicable but it's also important to reiterate it during the interview process when asked. Prior work experience will almost always be addressed.

Later in the interview, they asked my employment history. I had been unemployed since graduating from college and it was because of schizoaffective disorder. My employer asked if I had been employed the past 6 months and I simply informed her I've been searching for work but just haven't found anything yet. I had been out of school for a year but I withheld the information that I had graduated with schizoaffective disorder and that it was the reason I hadn't been working the prior 6 months.

She asked me where I've been looking and I simply replied I've been searching for entry level work just to get started and I want to move into management eventually. She asked me why I wanted to work in retail, and at the time, the main reasons were that I just needed to start a career and make some money. I told her I wanted to start a career and I also included some of the benefits I saw while applying for the position such as being on my feet and interacting with people. This was an instance where going beyond the response that directly answers the question and adding more to it helped me out.

Because she now knew I was qualified for the position another important part of interviewing is simply being yourself in a professional manner. Unless you're in a job with limited social interaction most human resources professionals are looking for people who are sociable and will interact well and get along with their employees. If they spot any potential problems they probably won't hire you regardless of your qualifications. In my experience using a little humor has been useful. It's also good to be personable while still observing the formality of the interview. Employers want to see you are a personable worker who will get along well with associates and customers and that you are also able to complete the work tasks.

Working at K-Mart after my second episode was important for me because it was a stepping stone. I knew I had a college degree and this wasn't the final destination but working a job where I was underemployed in a low stress environment helped me immensely. I hadn't worked for the previous year or so dating back to the beginning of my second episode and was still recovering from that second episode and I needed a job with simpler tasks and more socialization which K-Mart provided for me. During this first job, I learned how to reintegrate into society and how to interact with people in a work environment which helped me immensely in later jobs. I was also making some money and it boosted my self-esteem to know I was spending my time productively. I worked hard and felt good at the end of the day even though I felt I was underemployed. Two months later I applied for a job at Marriott International and was hired by someone

I grew up with. Having connections is always helpful in job searching and if you can network I strongly recommend it. Some people consider it nepotism, but I think if you are doing a good job after being hired then there's nothing to be ashamed of. Almost everyone catches a break from networking while advancing their career.

One of the most important things about obtaining a job is being able to say you have been working. To hiring managers, being employed tells them you are punctual, work well enough to hold a job, you're able to interact with others, and shows you are willing to work. When I applied from K-Mart to Marriott, having the K-Mart employment on my resume helped me. Unfortunately, I had to say I was underemployed, but I was able to inform them I took the job because I wanted to make money while searching for a different job instead of not working at all. If they think you're lazy the chances of getting hired are very slim.

In the past 5 years I've obtained 11 jobs and countless other interviews and have not been fired from any of those jobs. I was only asked to leave one of these jobs and it was a result of experiencing symptoms of my illness and having difficulty completing the work. I am fairly high functioning now but during the application process of many of those jobs I had a great deal of social anxiety. I still didn't disclose I have schizoaffective disorder and I still won't to this day. Most people won't make the assumption you have any disorders if you don't directly disclose this to them. They simply aren't aware of the way someone with schizophrenia or other mental disorders interact and they aren't capable of labeling the person as someone with something of this nature. This happens because they don't have the empirical knowledge to connect your behaviors to a diagnosis. Most people envision someone with a psychotic disorder the same way people are stigmatically portrayed in movies, so a little anxiety or awkwardness is almost never an indication of any mental disorders. If they see nervousness they usually assume it's because of the interviewing process, which does tend to create ten- sion and a little anxiety at times for most people, including those who haven't had a mental illness. This means if you detect they see nervousness it probably still means they are completely unaware you have any sort of diagnosis. Knowing this has kept me calm during interviews.

While being employed there have been times I've needed scheduling arrangements to attend doctor's appointments. I scheduled my doctor's appointments later in the day so I could still work a full day before them. There was an instance where a spreadsheet ask- ing for schedule arrangements was sent out, and I mis- took this as something only the administrator could read when it was available to everyone. Luckily, I put "I have doctor's appointments" and didn't elaborate and no one asked any questions.

I recommend going directly to the supervisor and just informing them you have doctor's appointments.

When I've done this I haven't been asked the reason and HIPPA regulations stipulate the employee isn't required to disclose their illness. If you're asked the reason for the appointments you can just provide a doctor's note. I've never been asked to disclose an illness directly, but sometimes it's asked indirectly and you still don't need to state it and can't be fired or disciplined at all for not doing so.

As I mentioned, I moved around in employment a great deal. In college, I worked for a grounds crew and that made my day easier because I was around people who had similar interests as me, and I was doing work which appealed to my nature. Being around baseball during college summers was a lot of fun because I love the game.

After working at K-Mart I worked for Marriott, an Insurance Company, I landscaped, worked more hospitality, worked for a pharmaceutical company, a customer service company, a bank, and several other places. I spent a lot of time searching for the right place to work and just wasn't able to find something I was satisfied with. After leaving the Insurance Company, I went to grad school shortly but decided against teaching English. I still knew I loved English and was unemployed and out of school. Instead of spending the money I had saved and idling away, I used my unemployment time wisely and I went to the library and studied writing 5 days a week and read good literature for countless hours to improve my literacy and writing ability. The unemployment lasted 5–6 months and I worked towards becoming a writer the entire time.

I enrolled in a writing class and was invited to a writing group which I still attend to this day.

To pursue writing I needed a job that was less intellectual so I could come home from work and be mentally able to read and write. Previously, I returned home from administrative work and my mind was too exhausted to read or write much of anything. I knew I was going to be sacrificing money for happiness but the point of having money is to be happy. I am working my way through the ranks to become a butcher and/or manager at the shop and I currently work full time and I have been pursuing writing in my spare time. I have felt good about working at the butcher shop because I enjoy the work and the high volume of social interaction. Although I haven't had as much money I've been extremely happy with my decision.

The decision was important because it has allowed me to do what I want with my life. I've had a Theodore Roosevelt quote on my door for some time stating it's important to dare greatly because " ... At best (those who dare) know the triumph of high achievement, but at worst if they fail, they do so while daring greatly, so they'll never be amongst those cold and timid souls who know neither victory nor defeat." This quote has resonated strongly with me and I decided I can't look back on my life and ask myself, "What would my life have been like if I decided to pursue writing?" Every day I write I feel satisfied with the decision I made and the effort I've expended toward pursuing my goals.

Losing Weight With Mental Health Struggles - A
Holistic Approach
Good Men Project, October 2019

After two episodes of schizoaffective disorder I was fairly depressed and exhausted. I was
taking psychiatric medications which sapped my
energy and I also had some trauma from having
nearly starved to death. At age 22 during my first
hospitalization I weighed 125 lbs and during my
second episode at age 24 I weighed 145 lbs. I'm
five foot nine with a stocky frame and when I'm
healthy I'm around 200 lbs. I will preface this article
by saying the methods used to lose weight in this
article worked for me but it's probably best to check
with your doctor to see what might work for you.

After my episodes, eating was one of my
immediate coping skills for negative emotions. I
would eat exorbitantly and wasn't certain why. For
years my weight waxed and waned and at age 32 I
had weighed 236 lbs for four years which was well
overweight. I decided I needed to do something to
become healthier.

At first there were many psychological bar-
riers in the way. During my episodes I had a delusion that I had to eat less so that everyone could

have more food which in turn would prevent world famine. I thought I was a messiah and my thoughts were being broadcasted so if I did this everyone else in the world would too. I had to refute this thought, even though in the present day I was rational enough to see that it wasn't true or rational, and address my fear of losing weight. Having lost a ton of weight in the past made it scary to event think about losing weight. I told myself I could lose ten pounds at a time and then level out and keep repeating this process. This provided some alleviation but it was still scary to think about losing more weight. I still worried I would get into bad habits of losing too much weight and I wouldn't be able to stop it, as had happened in the past. I addressed this fear to some extent and partially refuted it which was helpful. I figured I should be able to lose weight without losing too much weight but the prospect was still scary. It took a leap of faith to transcend this fear and there was no particular time where I felt one hundred percent ready. I decided it's now or never and I'm going for it.

The first step I took was eating healthier. I tried several small adjustments in my diet which had small effects but my weight remained the same. After listening to a research presentation by

Professor Dost Ongur of Harvard Medical School I decided I needed to substantially reduce the amount of starches, carbohydrates, and sugars in my diet but not entirely eliminate them. In his presentation he sited there is evidence for a significant population of people with psychosis that breaking down carbohydrates and sugars in the brain can be more difficult for you and this slows down cognition. Therefore not putting simple carbs and sugars into your body has proven effects of improving cognition for a significant amount of the population of people who have experiences with psychosis. I started doing an abbreviated version of the Keto diet where I would have some bread and sugar but not much. At first I felt cravings for the carbs and sugars which was difficult emotionally and mentally. My brain was strained at first and I felt depressed and stressed. Once my body adjusted I noticed I felt better emotionally, I had more energy, and I did notice some improvements in my clarity of thought. Seeing these results in my mental and emotional health motivated me to keep doing this diet. Along with this I lost 16 pounds which was a substantial amount of weight.

Another part of losing the weight was not eating as much in the morning. The struggle I had was that in my episodes one of the driving factors for mania was starvation. I would be starving at night and wouldn't be able to sleep because of it. Flight or fight instincts would kick in giving me an enormous amount of adrenaline at night as my body was desiring food thus keeping me awake. This experience has caused me to be more of a night time eater. It's been a habit I've become better with but I decided not to fight it immediately. There's research stating from primal times the human body is accustomed to going one to two days without food. Having heard this I decided I would not eat until lunch time every day. I couldn't prevent myself from eating at night but I didn't feel hunger in the morning therefore that was the time I picked to fast. Fasting in the mornings has also helped me to maintain my weight.

I started trying to exercise more but I didn't have the motivation. For years I had blamed the medication for not having motivation to exercise. In recent years as I've alleviated most of the experiential burdens of the trauma of schizoaffective disorder I learned that most of that exhaustion is not from the medication. Most of the exhaustion came from maladaptive thoughts and behaviors I had adopted to cope with the enormous amount of stress I was carrying with me through every day. This can be different from person to person but for myself I taken the same low dose of medication I've been on for eight years. As I have gained increasingly more alleviation from stress I've had more energy to exercise and my cognition has also improved. Having more energy was helpful but there was more that needed to be done.

After improving my health enough mentally and emotionally I still struggled with exercise. I had a gym membership and lived five minutes away but I wasn't going. I decided I needed to make exercise more fun and I started golfing more. I was playing indoor golf twice a week and once the weather improved I played more outdoor golf. Eventually realizing I wasn't going to the gym I canceled the membership and put the money from the monthly membership towards golf. At first I struggled with financing golf and it was incredibly frustrating. However, I had a stroke of luck and walked nine holes at six am one morning. They only charged fifteen dollars for the early bird special and I live in the Greater Boston area. This was a gift, as golf was now affordable for me. Most clubs have an early bird special if you're willing to wake up early enough. I also started doing two dumbbell exercises per day at home and sticking to this routine. I thought two exercises was doable time-wise and also very accessible as the dumbbells were in my bedroom. This helped but another thing I also started doing was building more walking into my day. I would take the stairs at work which helped and on my lunch break I intentionally took longer walks to the cafeteria.

With a combination of all these things I lost about five more pounds. This is currently my process and I feel a lot healthier at this point. Ayurvedic practice is rooted in utilizing an innumerable amount of spices to provide nourishment and nutrition and to heal the mind and body. I originally thought just changing one or two things was all I needed to do lose weight. After making a number of changes I've lost 21 lbs in five months, I feel much healthier and I have more muscle too. I'm going to continue to work on more ways to incorporate healthy living into my life as the benefits have been very noticeable mentally, emotionally, and physically.

Facing Fears; If Medication Runs Out
Schizophrenia Bulletin by Oxford Medical Journals,
January 2018

Before beginning this essay I would like to say I haven't missed my medication in five years and I don't plan on skipping it at all and if I did I would consult my doctor first however, the following information has brought me peace of mind which was its' sole purpose.

One of the most stressful thoughts I've had in recent years has been wondering what my life would be like without medication. I've had schizoaffective disorder for ten years, five of which I've spent in episodes. During these episodes I was unable to function without my medication. I had neurosis, psychosis to the point where I couldn't carry an intelligible conversation, insomnia which seemed to be the genesis of all my problems, and crippling stress which triggered a number of other symptoms such as auditory and visual hallucinations. The past five years have been the ones where I've made the most progress and done the most recovery work but wondering if my life would fall apart without medication always burdened me.

Attacking this issue was important because I felt I had a dependency on something that I one day may or may not have access to. This was a situation where I thought out the scenarios and it brought me a huge amount of relief. I realized the way I function with medication now is completely different than when I first started taking it after my episodes. The dose hasn't changed so it was relieving to think that the person I am today may be more or less the same type of person I would be without medication. I worried I would never be able to sleep but I figured I would be able to make plans for gaining rest. Some of it may involve melatonin or a different sleep medication or increased exercise but I would find a way. I also worked on reducing stress which was previously inhibiting my sleep. For the past five years I haven't missed one night's rest due to being properly medicated. I realized I've worked on five notebooks worth of problems which had been hampering me which means I've already done a great deal of stress relief. I also noticed when I fall asleep without medication I am sometimes able to sleep at least six hours which was a relief to know.

One of the bigger issues I was facing in my subconscious was paranoia from my episodes.

During my episodes it seemed like everyone was out to get me but I realized that was not the case and would not be the case if I did in fact have to go without medication. I determined the reason they all looked worried or concerned was because of my state of being. Watching people who were disconcerted during interactions caused me to be so too but I've realized if I was in better health the way I am today this wouldn't necessarily be a problem because the interactions would be smoother and more functional. If I was in a good state of mind/being they wouldn't necessarily be disconcerted and exude it. I've gained a great deal of socialization skills which I never previously had and also wisdom to guide me through social situations which I was also lacking. These skills and wisdom would help me to maintain good mental health because I would know how to socialize and interact if I didn't have my medication. It would reduce or eliminate psychosis and I've realized the reduction and elimination of a number of symptoms may not necessarily have anything to do with the medication. The medication has served as a buffer to give me enough relief where I can live a functional life and work on issues however, the elimination of those issues has been a result of the work I've put forth in therapy, journaling, and writing. This means my work would not simply be erased and brought back to scratch if I was unable to gain access to my medication.

I also figured I wouldn't be in the same living situation that I was at school where I was losing weight to the point where I was 125 lbs when first hospitalized when I normally weigh 200 while healthy. During my work I routed out delusions such as having to be a messiah who would save the world and do so by eating less food so others could have more, not buying non-fair trade products, and reducing my carbon foot print as much as I possibly could beyond the point of reason. These were inhibiting delusions which put me in a living state where I was basically homeless. The other things I realized are that I've done a great deal of work with OCD which was originally cumbersome to the point where my hands were cut and bleeding from all the times I had been washing them during the day. I also had a number of other disabling routines which would be pretty much out of the mix.

Knowing what my triggers are was also an important component of alleviating the burden of possibly not having medication. During my episodes and earlier years I wasn't aware of the stimuli and situations which were causing symptoms and catalyzing episodes but now that I'm aware of what these are I feel if I didn't have my medication I would have an idea of how to limit my symptoms. I know that reading other people's writing at length has been a trigger so I could simply read less. I'm also aware that certain social situations used to create a ton of stress thus triggering symptoms. I learned my symptoms are controllable and it hasn't necessarily been the medication that has been the factor keeping them at bay. It's been gaining and furthering my knowledge of my illness and having coping strategies for the illness and symptoms. This was empowering to know because I realized I've been reducing the efficacy of my symptoms and the power it used to have over me through conscious decisions, actions, and learning rather than just through taking medication.

I learned that there also are a number of people who have schizophrenia and or bipolar disorder and they're living functional lives without medication. I never plan on going off my meds however this was proof that if medication somehow becomes unavailable to me it doesn't mean I'm going to lose everything that I've worked for. I do believe I would still maintain a good group of friends, I'd be able to do things like golf and shoot pool, I'd probably still be able to work in some capacity at some place, and I would also be able to at least lecture if not continue to write. Knowing I would still have a life worth while was the most important real-ization I made; understanding that the work that was done was facilitated by the medication but it was more so a product of reorganizing my mind through talk therapy, facing fears and delusions, developing my intelligence and cognitive skills, and putting forth work which will continue to serve me well even if one of my greatest fears comes to fruition. "Fear not, the things we are afraid of are bound to happen, however when they do, we'll find that there was nothing to fear." (John McMurray) This piece of wisdom also gives me hope after hav-ing written this essays.

Psychiatric Meds - Tips and Anecdotes

In terms of medication, these are the things that have worked for me. I'm uncertain whether they can or will work for anyone else but if they're of interest, I recommend consulting your doctor, psychiatrist, and/or prescriber first.

After my first hospitalization, overmedication caused me to sleep twelve to fourteen hours per day, I couldn't work, and I had no social life. I was lethargic and my personality was subdued, my vitality was lacking, and I couldn't feel very many emotions and even when I did they were not within the same ranges they had been at before my episodes. My stream of consciousness was slow and muddled, and my overall quality of life was really poor. Only several months after my first episode I was on vacation with my family and I felt that completely not being medicated gave me more of a life than being medicated so I quit the meds cold turkey. It's important to realize that not every psychiatrist is going to be a proponent of not taking meds or even of decreasing them but there are some who are, or who will at least let you try doing so and learning whether this may or may not work. For me, I had to learn on my own terms that I needed the meds and unfortunately, this is what it takes sometimes. It's been a helpful lesson in retrospect. Some psychiatrists will taper the meds in a safe manner but coming off the meds cold turkey can be a dangerous thing. It's important to remember psychiatrists are people too and it's good to have someone who is willing to listen to you.

Looking back I think it's easy to see how I came to the decision of quitting the meds. I wasn't given any other options for medication and I was suffering immensely from the side-effects. The side-effects were worse than the symptoms at that point in terms of my quality of life. After this I had a second episode and resulting in my second and last hospitalization. This time the medication type was different and it was a lower dose. After several months out of the hospital I still had some symptoms which was difficult to handle but I was able to work, have a social life, and sleep a reasonable number of hours. I had my sense of humor, my stream of consciousness wasn't at its' best but it was functional, and I could feel emotions. Experiencing symptoms was difficult but ultimately, being able to do the things I wanted in life motivated me to continue taking medication. I went to therapy on a weekly basis to talk about symptoms and issues I was having and although those problems were painful and difficult to navigate they were still bearable due to having a better and more reasonable quality of life.

In the beginning, I pushed away the thought of symptoms and I didn't want to work on my mental health. However, after a while, I realized that medication is not the only part of getting healthier. The medication stabilized me but it was therapy that gave me back my life. Over the years I've had a myriad of issues arise with my mental health, but working through them has been the key to getting healthier and staying out of the hospital. In terms of cognition, intelligence, character, and functionality, I've completely transformed over the past nine years and it's been due to therapy as well as continuing the meds. Taking low doses was a part of this. Had I not been subjected to the symptoms I don't think I would have had avenues to get to the roots of the problems causing the psychosis. Most of my psychosis has been experiential while I believe some of it is biological, so being subjected to the symptoms forced me to work through the issues causing the problems. It was a difficult road but I have my life back and I'm living a good life. In earlier years I thought my exhaustion, slow cognition, and subdued emotions were from the medication however, as I worked through increasingly more issues these things improved immensely. Phenomenon I originally thought were side-effects of meds were being caused by the experiential side of the illness.

Switching gears, the rest of the article has to do with some helpful stories around meds. A few years back I was home sick from work with flu-like symptoms and I took an anti-histamine based medication which mixed poorly with my anti-psychotic. It caused me an ear-splitting headache, dizziness and nausea and I couldn't work that day. After calling the pharmacy I learned these meds don't mix well. The pharmacist can cross reference medications in their systems that will tell you whether you can take any combination of medications together. I've realized that asking about this in person could divulge that I'm taking an anti-psychotic and there could be people around whom I didn't want knowing about my mental health so it made sense to call in advance to have the pharmacy cross reference the meds. Your psychiatrist should also have a sense of whether over the counter meds will mix well or not with your current meds.

Another issue I had more recently was having difficulty with prescriptions for an ear infection. I went to a reputable medical center and stopped in to their urgent care where I was prescribed a steroid for my ear. I wasn't able to fill the prescription that morning which worked to my advantage. Luckily, I had a meeting with my psychiatrist, who is also my therapist, that night after work before getting the prescription. He looked at the prescription and mentioned that the 50 mg of a steroid I was prescribed can induce psychosis and mania and that it was poor prescribing. He also mentioned how he's had several other patients who had this same experience and it flared up their mental health symptoms and they were hospitalized. I was fairly furious and a little scared at the poor prescribing. My psychiatrist mentioned he tends to see this when people are in healthier states. For some reason to some prescriber's this potentially inclines them to disregard the psychiatric diagnosis which is listed in their medical notes which they read before seeing you. Another part of me wonders if the prescriber just wasn't aware of how steroids can induce psychosis and mania if you have a predisposition towards those ailments. Going forward, my psychiatrist mentioned to email him any time I'm given new prescriptions to prevent things of this nature from happening.

One of the difficulties of taking meds has been the exhaustion in the mornings. About six years ago, I added an anti-anxiety medication that I was supposed to take in the morning. After taking it, I was too exhausted to work out. I've recently realized I can delay taking it on the weekends so I can get a workout in first. Getting in the workout has helped with my mental and emotional health and once I get home from a walk or I'm done lifting weights I usually take it afterwards.

With my psychiatrist's guidance, it also helped to tamper with the meds a little and try different doses to optimize their efficacy. In the beginning I was afraid of increasing the anti-psychotic even the slightest bit. I had such a bad experience with being over-medicated that I was afraid of changing anything. Also, I was very low on energy and I was afraid I'd be even more depleted but increasing the medication was helpful. After adding one mg I was pretty happy with the way I felt and with the improvement in the way I was functioning. A year or so later we added an anti-anxiety medication, which I was reluctant to do, and for the first time in years I felt like myself. It was tough to face the fear of adding meds after having had such a bad experience with them but it definitely helped.

I also struggled with thinking the medication was making me tired, drowsy, depressed, slow minded. After having made progress in therapy I realized that most of these negative symptoms had more to do with the experiential side of the illness. As I dismantled the thought webs that were afflicting me, my cognitive and emotional health began improving. Over the years, I've taken the same amount of medication and my cognition is quicker than ever, I feel better emotionally, I have more energy, and a good portion of this is due to alleviating the burdens of trauma from the experiential side of the illness. I originally thought those side-effects were entirely meds but more of them had to do with the illness than the medication.

For a while, I felt like the medications were making me hungry all the time as well as tired. After discovering I was lactose intolerant and having had some GI issues I had to change my diet. Before changing my diet I was eating a lot of processed foods and I was constantly hungry. I never felt like the food was satiating my appetite. I had to switch to whole, plain foods and I transformed the way I ate to eat as healthy as possible. I cut out sugar, I ate fruits and vegetables, and I utilized healthy fats like olive oil, coconut, avocado, and oat milk. Switching to a healthier diet curbed my appetite, thus making me realize what I originally thought was hunger due to medications, had more to do with eating processed foods. Processed foods have chemicals in them that are designed to make you hungrier which was something I realized after I stopped eating them. Along with this my energy levels increased and some of my brain fog went away. These were all things I thought were side-effects of the medications when it was partly diet.

Medication; A Sequence of Events

Recently, I made an attempt to stop taking medication and to see how well I would feel. It's been something I've been working towards for many years. Although the effort was unsuccessful there was a lot I
learned during the process.

In my efforts to stop taking medication I first
started with my anxiety medication. I take it six days per
week so it retains its' effect. The first two days off the
medication I still felt okay. By the third day I noticed
substantial differences in my ability to think clearly and
verbalize my thoughts. I felt more energy and I was
sleeping less which incentivized me to keep going, but I
knew I couldn't keep going with the level of cognition I
was at. I followed this by trying to take it every other
day but this also wasn't working. In the beginning of my
mental health journey I always had the notion that if I
could become healthy enough I could come off my medication, so having this experiment seemingly fail was
really disheartening. However, there was still good that
came from stopping my meds and then coming back on
them. I did realize that even without the medication I
was still healthy enough to function well enough to get

by, maybe not in the line of work I'm currently in or with the same quality of cognition but this was a helpful realization. I always had the fear that if I somehow just wasn't able to access medication that I'd completely digress into a state of full out psychosis. This question still remains somewhat unanswered as I didn't try coming off the psychosis-based meds but it was helpful to know I'm still somewhat functional without the anxiety meds. It also informed me that I should potentially keep a back up supply of some of the anxiety medication if I can in case for some reason I can't reach the pharmacy and it's not accessible.

After this failure I had a ton of resentment for the situation I was in. I realized that the illness probably isn't going to leave me and I'm going to need medication for the rest of my life. This was incredibly difficult to bare and I felt a cauldron of negative emotions within my heart and body. After stewing in this concoction of negativity, I came to a higher realization. Regardless of where I'm at with my mental health. I don't want to harbor these emotions anymore. It's the negative emotions that are causing me to feel terrible and not necessarily the dysfunction of the brain when I don't have medication. It's my emotions towards the illness and towards the things I've been through that is truly the sickness within me that just needs to go. This desire to expunge negativity motivated me to keep thinking through my illness and the causes of negativity within me.

During this trial period of not having anxiety medication I also noticed I wasn't fully engaged in conversations and I didn't know how to respond within a conversation or how to be on the same page as everyone. This took me back to my years growing up where I had felt the same way. It gave me clarity into the fact that I was not on the same page as everyone growing up and this led to a lot of bullying. It also gave me a sense that the comments I was making when I wasn't up to par this time were not really comments that set people up to even give positive responses to. Although it's still the bullies' faults for treating me poorly it allowed me to be more forgiving of them because I had better insight into the ways my comments were probably landing when I was growing up and how far off the beaten path they were. This didn't make the bullying right but it at least made it understandable that maybe I wasn't making comments that were easy to respond to. Also, for years I had blamed

myself for all the bullying I had experienced, thinking there was some sort of morality involved in my
inability to connect socially and that it was entirely
my fault. However, I realized that maybe it was just
biological. When I do have medication I'm able to
function on the same level as everyone I talk to in
just about any situation whether it's work, dating,
social gatherings, and people of all walks of life as
well. Even during my younger years I took some
medication for a short period of time and my life
was completely different during those months. The
insight I gained into how my mind works without
medication led to a major improvement in my mental health. I realized that I'm probably not going to
be able to change my brain's biology, but if I continue to take medication I'll be fine.

More importantly, after having years of re-
sent for the bullying I experienced in middle school
and while pledging I gained new insight. I realized if
my mind wasn't working well during those times the
persons who were doing the bullying probably were
not their best selves as well. I learned that it would
be easier to just let go of the past and to let them
off the hook rather than harbor resentment and hatred for the things they did. The ability to under-

stand that maybe their minds were not in their best states either and that they may have been struggling mentally and emotionally helped me to forgive them. The ability to forgive also led me to another point. I learned the source of the negative emotions was resentment and hatred for all the struggles and trauma I've been through over the years with my two episodes of schizoaffective disorder, pledging the frat, and going through middle school. I found a great emotional burden was lifted when I made the decision to let go of the anger I had towards people for the way they treated me. I also was able to see more clearly that maybe some of those situations had more gray to them than I thought. In middle school I definitely didn't mistreat anyone but it's become easy enough to forgive the other kids from a vantage point of knowing that growing up is a difficult thing and no one really knows what they're doing during that time even though we all pretend we do. I could barely speak a coherent sentence to stand up for myself during that time because I was so beaten down from everyone's disparagement. As far as pledging I could see how the fraternity guys were probably messed up from having gone through the same process of pledging they were putting me through. Seeing this helped me to somewhat exonerate them and to help let go of all the wrong they did. I think overall just letting go of the anger and resentment towards the illness and all the struggles I have been through was the biggest takeaway in this sequence of events. It told me there's still work I need to do with my years in the frat and pledging but at least taking away the burden of hatred has been extremely helpful. "Hatred, which could destroy so much, never failed to destroy the man who hated, and this was an immutable law"(James Baldwin).

Made in United States
Orlando, FL
04 April 2023

31745269R00136